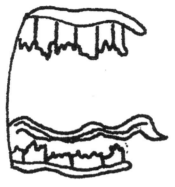

suicide nOtes
the short works of
christopher brett bailey
stories , poems , routines
text collages , vocal tics & verbal diarrhoea

OBERON BOOKS
LONDON

WWW.OBERONBOOKS.COM

First published in 2018 by Oberon Books Ltd
521 Caledonian Road, London N7 9RH
Tel: +44 (0) 20 7607 3637 / Fax: +44 (0) 20 7607 3629
e-mail: info@oberonbooks.com
www.oberonbooks.com

A catalogue record for this book is available from the British Library.

PB ISBN: 9781786825278
E ISBN: 9781786825285

Cover doodle by the author
Cover layout by Jamie Hewitt

eBook conversion by Lapiz Digital Services, India.

CONTENTS

DAIRY MILK DRAG QUEENS

dairy milk drag queens, sucking breast milkshakes in the parking lot of an upstate dairy queen. chem trails streak the sky above us like toxic money shots, at the climax of a government porno for military mind control. 'don't breathe in faggot, that's how they get you.' flecks of ice cream lipstick dribble off my chin. as night arrives to save us, knight arrives on horseback, and night pulls out and frignatures his way across a whore's back. the last embers of a suburban sun tan flicker SOS from heaven all the way to right here. we 3 drag queens take drags on mentholated charcoal, all square jaws and stubbly legs dressed to 9's 10's and 11's in illegal-high-heels and screaming low cut dresses. sunflower patterns with open mouths, shouting 'i may not be in fashion this season rick but i cling to a man's cleavage like disease clings to his speckled dick' and i wish i were an angel, doc, i wish i was dead. cause i'd float up from this tailgate party, huffing chem trails all the way, having chem sex with an angel or 2 in the queue. for st peter's check-in desk, with a pearl necklace so long i'd have to wrap it round twice, one jizz jewel from every good man that i blew. there'd be a pearl from you and you and even from you. 'i'm glad to be offa that sodden hydro stone, st penis' i'd say tipping my halo like a hat … they ain't nothing but a bunch of wet babies with a liquid addiction. blood, come, milk, sweat, pus, venereal discharge. it's just one juice after another with those goddamn humans. what's wrong with being dry? don't you like it rough? what have you got against friction? blood, come, milk, canadian ginger ale – there isn't a liquid on this planet i haven't ejaculated. i can ejaculate most anything. i ejaculated breakfast this morning, veggie sausage roll, banana loaf (organic) and a cup of strong coffee. irony is i take mine without the cream. passed a homeless in the street ejaculated him enough coins to buy a sandwich and two extra to leave a tip. once you've passed a two pound coin through your man clit a gal stone is a cinch. show me a guy stressing about a gal stone and i'll show you a guy who needs his japanese eyesocket stretched by a lubricated hex key. that ain't folklore. depends who your folks are, you can find 'em doing it … singles night in the search bar: j-a-p-s. i. japs eye. or as my japanese friends call it? my eye. who's thirsty? i think i feel an ejaculation coming on.

and the doctor unfolds a hinged pointer, his laser eye surgically scanning the room for an apt pupil. 'here' he gestures, towards a tin bathtub under fluorescent lights, in which severed testicles float on a calm lake of saline solution like archipela-gonads clustered off the coastline of a country just out of shot. and the camera pans, or rather zooms, as it's strapped to the nose of a drone. 'here' he repeats 'here float the nutsacks of innocent boys. popping 'em off with garden implements and over the counter anaesthetics, desperate to step out of the inevitable march of fast forward progress, the infinite boot falling line after line after line as this species spurts its way towards a planet so saturated with human beings you can't fart freely without fear of putting a midget off his lunch. we will not go forth and multiply, we will not go forth and multiply, you can't make us, they're saying by their 1000s as their genitals roll to the floor like ping pong balls at a thalidomide table tennis tournament' and while he said this i went booze-woozy but i'd had no lush for lunch. i was mommy funeral sober and living in stoic veneration of the venerabullshit in front of me, but here i was in the midst of a full-blown hallucination city, yellow sky taxis swerving with lizard skin upholstery. red, green stop lights like floating popsicles in front of me on tiny streets of my own imagining. don't let these tiny cars floating in front of your eyes like dandruff dust particles by gaslamp flip your lid kid. flip your lid kid. it's your own invention. shut yr eyes doc. shut yr eyes doc. be patient. shut yr eyes. so i did. and they burned red against black behind my puppy dog lids: all the roads i'd ever run down. all the roads that had run me over, tire cut me in half, intestines snaking out of my torso like i'm giving birth to a stillborn medusa. all the roads i know: the i-90, the new jersey turnpike, traffic jams on the m4 the m5 and the M I 666. police chief died today, throat slit by a satanist youth cult high on fast drugs and slow heavy metal, who will our little boys look up to now gov? so i jump in one of those little taxi cabs made of dandruff and i whistle 'yo homie smell ya later' in a reference i start to wonder if i'm the wrong colour to make. cause if you could choose to be chocolate you wouldn't choose to be white chocolate. and part of me's still at that dairy queen saying 'ya ever notice how thirsty you get after a milkshake? it's definitely less of a drink and more of a dessert' and by now the taxi has tunnelled deep on a freeway,

constricted by brain cell phones and glass block new builds
on every side. the driver licks his lips in the rearview, his loins
wet from engine coolant. i lick my lips back at him – part from
politeness, part from milkshake stains – his left eye goes to wink
and BAMMM telephone pole came outta nowhere, steering
column through his chest, radio blaring a CB flirtation from
some trucker called nemonic to an ex war zone nurse braggin
about her freshly pierced clitoris, KKKSSSSHHHH – i turn
the radio dial – Top Ten drum solos that aren't drum solos: in at
number one the sound of police nightstick on inmate dick. Bang
Bang Bang Bang Bang. 'You know why you're in here? You
know why you're in here? You know why you're in here? You
know why you're in here? You know why you're in here? repent
you scumbag. i don't want you to pent i want you to pent again.'
the cop on the radio is bleating away and i'm outta the car by
now, running round the backside, i pop open the trunk. looking
for a tire pump or whatever – i don't know what i expected to
find, driver's manual, or … there's this suitcase. your suitcase.
picture it. the one you take on holiday. on vacation. maybe
there's still those airline ribbon paper n glue things with airport
codes on 'em. maybe's there's not. and it smells like you, this
bag. so i know it's yours. i huh unzip it and inside is um. is your
clothes. your clothing. the clothes you're wearing now, and the
clothes you had on yesterday and at the beginning of the week.
and i pick them up, and they. there's this smell that just. like.
wafts off them. they're wet. they smell of sweat and they stink. all
the white clothes are stained where the toxins are coming out in
your perspiration, like panic sweat. like not. normal. sweat. and
they stink gently of what you ate today, and this week, what you
put in your body, and there's shit runs in the trousers and silk
come or vag streaks in the crotch. lightweight heavy petting, i
think i smell, discharge, inhale, and i think i smell me. my sweat,
my ejaculate. i breathe deep and i blush to tell you this, a movie
flickers behind my eyelids: what we did. what you and i did.
what i did when i got in you. what you begged me to. what you
begged me to. what you begged me to. what you begged me not
to. don't stop. don't stop. don't stop. don't stop. don't stop. don't
stop. don't stop. don't stop. don't stop. don't don't don't don't
don't don't don't don't don't don't don't stop stop stop stop
stop stop stop stop stop stop stop stop stop stop stop stop stop.

beg me i said
beg me with one single tear
and your duct fucked out two drops
so you got a strike across your face
blood pissed from the cut
i pressed my thumb up to it, to stop the flow,
and i gripped your baby head in my wide open hand,
do you love me? i said
and your other duct released a single tear
and that takes control.

PORNOGRAPHIC NEWSREEL

pornographic newsreel in endless tape loo/
pornographic newsreel in endless tape loo/
pornographic newsreel in endless tape loo/
pornographic newsreel in endless tape loo/
pornographic newsreel in endless tape loo/
pornographic newsreel in endless tape loo/
n endless tape, endless tape, graphic newsreel
in endless tape, pornographic newsreel in ...
tape come splattered 1/4 inch disintegration loops, newsreel in
endle ...

tape running offa one spool and onto another. forever, flickering
images: sunspot burnt like speedball overdose, tape wearing thin
on the part we keep rewinding over.
stop, here comes playhead: hot tongues licking warm wounds,
open sores on burnt flesh, burnt flesh is flesh of prepubescent
boy-whore, ... dried pus and blood-sick saliva, treacle thick
and grenadine red ... his is a body fucked twice – once by a
landmine and once by every horny soldier in this goddamn
battalion. – no limbs, just a torso n neck, face down in the dust,
flies circle making landing strip of sunburned back. scabs piled
like control towers. soldier milk streaked like aeroplane oil leak,
mixing with pus. soldier squints and kicks sun out of his eyes, 'I
think he's finally dead.'
torso flinches, fear rippling up spine, or maybe relief, as if to say
as if to say 'not quite'. soldier mounts boy-whore, dirty rectum
fecal soft membrane hugs the quivering meatus. soldier fires
off another round in record time. as the last volt of electricity
blinkers out of the boy's power tubes: close-up on a bead of
sweat, maybe a tear. less likely to be rain.
but the two faces are caught fish-eyed in a tiny water glob
reflection – one looks like me

click off the tapehead, run the footage again ...

and one looks like you. who you wanna play tonight and just
who's playing who?

sweat bubbles out of navel, soft cock stuffed back into unzipped
khakis, military issue, longshot: sun high, jeep radio blares
distorted action plan, boy torso, one arm dangling off.

ffwd – i hate this part –

bead of sweat, maybe a tear, less likely to be rain –

back a minute – *back* –

soldier mounts boy-whore, dirty rectum fecal soft membrane
hugs the quivering meatus. soldier pumps, grinds, leans back
for better angle. working deeper thrusts for another round. no
record time this time. this time can't finish. boy-whore torso
sighs, exacerbated, like 'hurry up'. soldier looks deflated, ego
struck, what a bossy bottom. cock softening, boy-whore torso
lying limp, soldier closes eyes for concentration … hardening,
hardening, sorta, but can't quite – softening … 'err. i can't do it
again. not so soon.' soldier stares down lens of camera into our
living room …

you and me shrug, cocks in hand

torso says 'sheesh don't prolong this ya'll'

soldier says 'shut up' and raises fist

you say 'don't kill him, man, if you kill him first none of us come
… we learned that the hard way last time …'

soldier wipes brow, resigned, he knows you are right

i switch hands, pump soft and wonder if your 'the hard way' pun
was intentional. decide it probably was not.

hardening, the soldier squeezes, blood runs from face, tightening
legs, sand licking up onto scabs, rectum drinking cock in,
hopeful bead of pre-cum bubble kisses anal pus in petri wetness
desert hate dish. the tape reels whir. soldier fires off another
round in record time, as the last volt of electricity blinkers out
of the boy's power tubes. bead of sweat, maybe a tear. less likely
to be rain. close-up on bead of liquid; in it two faces are caught
fish-eyed but clear, – one looks like me and the other like you –
a portrait of us in a tiny water glob reflection. us, holding hands

like first date lovebirds, seed drying our palms together. mine to
yours, filmy white puddle, like elmers school glue.

click off the tapehead, run the footage again …

THE POO-ICIDE

2001,
buffalo, new york

go your own way / go your own way-a-yay / call it my love / everyday
breaking the law / breaking the law /
bass how low can you go? death row? /
young gifted and /
hot time summer in the city back on my neck getting dirt and gritty /
and experts are calling this the / ever / what do you think about that
callers? /

cop car sped along the road, ran a red light by accident. fuck it
what's immunity for she thought, rolling down her window and
screaming 'wahoo – i love this city!'
kim rex was the youngest lady cop to ever make detective and
sporter of the second shortest crew cut on the force. her bic'd
scalp bounced light like a skin disco ball but was no match for
the hairless dome of lieutenant skip santiago. santiago had been
scalped in a casino raid in '96 and got the top of his head re-
plastered with melted plastics. now he shampoos as normal and
conditions with furniture polish. some say parts of his brain were
still exposed during the surgery and that the plastics dripped
down into his mind ... the toxins enabling him to think faster.

kim rex didn't know too much about that but she did know that
santiago was a darn fast thinker. nobody wanted to play chess
with him because he'd finished his side of the game before you'd
made your first move.

/ cshhooowaa / blurted the police radio –
yeah, rex here ... i got a call about a rumpus between i90 and
the 104. i wanna see what's shaking over there / CSHH / yeah
i know it's way below my pay grade but i'm in the hood, what
am i gonna do drive *around* the problem? / CSHH / okay, tough
guy. i love you too.

this was her sign off with all the male cops. it drove them *in*sane.

cop car sped on and on. towards that rumpus by the i90.

meanwhile back at the station officer chuck delaney who had
moments ago been on the other end of the police radio was
pushing a filing cabinet closed, the steel wheels running in their
tracks, when he looked down to find he was sporting an erection
the size of a pool cue. goddamnit, he thought. that detective
gets me so … *long*. he had no choice but to take a second lunch
break, go to the local pool hall and play pool with it.
he'd shark the good old boys out of their factory pensions.
'hey good old boys! 20 smackers says i can whoop you at
snooker with this cue in my shorts!'
'alright whippersnapper you're on …' grandpa had hit the sweet
spot between lively and intoxicated, so the shakes had levelled
out and he was feelin cocky. 'but before we proceed with this
tomfoolery, this barroom olympiad. what's got ya so long in the
shorts?'
'well, there's this new detective. gets me so hot – i see her blow
her nose i gotta take a cold shower.'
'i remember those feelings!' (nostalgia jostled with stigmatisms
for supremacy in his eye)
'well … why don't cha just take her?'
'it doesn't work like that anymore.'
'gosh this world is a-changing. you know how much a sandwich
used to cost?'
'that's not really what we're talking about.' delaney said thrusting
his mighty pool cue expertly. pre-cum spurting gently from its
chalky tip. he sank two balls in the side pocket.

cop car swerved to the side of the road. tears of joy are
streaming down the cheeks of detective kim rex. 'god i love my
job!' she screamed.
her mood tended to swing from good to gooder and she was
prone to the occasional bout of happy crying. god had gifted her
abnormally large tear ducts. water globules the size of lychees &

ping pong balls would come rolling out of her face and bound off her cheekbones like a ramp.

she sat alone in her cruiser crying joyfully.

she buttoned up her leather trench coat so her tears would not soak thru her top. 'this ain't a wet t-shirt contest' she said aloud. and then laughed like 'heeeh'.

'wait a minute – that's not my laugh. whose laugh is that? i've heard that laugh before. but it doesn't belong to me ...'

she narrowed her eyes like a good detective while her brain scanned for the answer.

1000s of laughs flashed before her ears. chuckles, chunters, grunts, guffaws. tv laughs, friends laughs, the laughs of lovers and dead lovers. the nervous laughter of suspects, colleagues. (laughs from childhood, from inside her mother, from past lives lived in far flung and long destroyed places)

meanwhile: cop car sped towards the crime scene.

detective kim rex squinted the setting sun out of her eyes, slipped butterfly shades onto her head

the tears dried to a salty film on her freckled cheeks.

the day did a dusk thing, the city glowed amber. olivia newton john woulda called it a summer night.

rubber burned hot to the road.

chainlink fences whizzed by, strip malls and corner stores. basketball courts, two churches, both charred to a crisp. boarded up windows from pipe bomb explosions, houses with graffiti for walls, cardboard windows and ransacked storefronts.

cop car began to slow

a rickety apartment building made of bamboo and limestone loomed.

the satellite navigation said 'this must be the place'.

detective kim rex killed the engine and kissed her tom tom on the cheek.

you're the most articulate boy i know, she said, laughing out loud to nobody.

'that's not my laugh ... whose laugh IS that?'

commissioner kacey calhoun was pacing on the bamboo
veranda. he was 6 ft 3, about 1000 years old, skin like peameal
bacon, face like a pan of boiling water. steam rose off him and
evaporated into the sticky afternoon. kacey was six months on
the wagon, and about to get found out for extortion, tax evasion,
child pornography, accepting bribes, corruption of justice. and
his nose made that out of tune trumpet noise when he blew it.
not a pleasant character. but none of that matters too much to
this story.

'welcome to the fucking scene, kimberly. what can i say … ? i'm
not happy to see you, this is above your paygrade. it's taken care
of. and unless you're the police photographer, you've got no
business at my crime scene.'

she stared him out. his face softened and his gob fell open:

'overdosed on laxatives. shat out his internal organs. looks like
he tried to shit out his rib cage, went n tore holes in himself like
a sprinkler. bones all protruding out of his ass like he's sitting
on a throne made of his own damn skeleton. bone throne, they
call it. third one this week. a veritable trend. the city is rife with
hopeless people shitting themselves to death. and this here
apartment is all coated in excrement of course. turds clinging
to every stick of furniture. stomach acid rotting the wallpaper
and discolouring the upholstery. whole place reeks of bile,
and there's half digested lunches and snacks clinging to the
lampshades and the light fixtures. it's a poopy mess in there, son.
you don't wanna see it. the first sergeants that got in there shat
themselves spontaneously, just on sight. like how when ya smell
another person's vomit it prompts you to do a little copycat
vomit of your own. well, much the same principle here i s'pose.
who knew detectives kane and wet were so weak of the colon?
we sent 'em home to change and shower and so forth, should be
back within the hour. meantime i radio'd the station for some
lackie to bring up adult diapers and SARS face masks just in
case. preventative action, that's 9/10ths of prevention. now, i'll
warn ya, this ain't no girly playing with barbie dolls n unicorns

kinda crime scene. there's 2 corpses in there ... one appears to be caucasian and the other one is just plain asian. caucasian i deduce is a friend, maybe lover, appears to have died of shock upon finding the first fella. either that or an amphetamine overdose. the heart has blown out, so i figure ...'

by this point the musculature of kim's face had morphed into the kind of sneer that spells out 'i pray they don't find a cure for cancer before it catches up with you. i won't send flowers.'

calhoun smiled. looked just like an asshole with bacon lips.

detective kim rex pushed past the ancient blowhard and into the crimescene.
just like she pictured: a slummy firetrap apartment.
no sunlight, jenga piles of styrofoam and cardboard. yellowing wallpaper, even the nicotine stains have nicotine stains. smashed bottles – possibly from a skirmish.
she kicks the bedroom door open, a lightbulb on a chain, tiny box room, every surface completely coated in turds. like fudgy mashed potato layered thick on the furniture, the ceiling, the back of the door.
and at the centre of it all? a confetti cannon of a corpse.
a 24 year old korean phd student, well turned out, well spoken, well ... not anymore. his whole lower half had been inverted from a dynamite laxative, blowing a bukshit hole through his midriff, colon-izing the whole room.
detective kim rex swallowed loudly.
a ball of sludge dripped off the ceiling fan in a long stringy stalactite. plop.
kim rex snapped on a plastic glove and held back vomit as she swiped two fingers along the wall. she rolled the sludge between thumb and forefingers. watched its consistency change, watched granules separate out then magically gloop back together.
forming and reforming on a loop.
she brought the latex hand to her face and sniffed: *sniff long*
'this shit isn't shit.' she said.

sniff short, sniff long
her steely eyes narrowed. her mouth chattered open. red lips in
disbelief.

the way the other corpse was lying didn't look right to rex. its
arm contorted at a right angle like it'd fallen from a great height.
people who die indoors don't die in this position. she lifted one
of its hands and wiped the shit off it. she used a lighter to burn
flesh off the pinkie finger, she plunged her fingertips inside to
feel up the bone. sure enough, just as she suspected: a graphite
skeleton.

she stormed back outta the house.
calhoun was sitting in a rocking chair on the porch now. legs
spread wide to imply a dangling dong. crust on his teeth like a
loaf of bread, menace in his eyes, his hand fingering the butt of
his pistol.

'this isn't a crime scene. it's a photoshoot.' rex howled.

'open and shit case. it's a poo-icide plain n simple. seems there's
some kind of laxative deathcult sweeping the nation. sweeping it
clean. with a thick bristled broom. just one sweep after another,
right across humanity. and every soul that's not glued down is
getting loosened up and swept away, right outta this life.'

'this is a counterfeit poo-icide, calhoun, and you know it. i could
smell a real one with my nose corked shut with baking soda.
what are you hiding? '

'nothing but my contempt for you, detective'. he said, standing
to his feet. every vertebrae in his bacon back crackling audibly
as he did so.

she kissed her teeth at him. *thht*

'you sure your teeth are the last thing you wanna kiss in this
world, tommy boy? you're walking feet first into a nightmare,

sugar tit. you're gonna come toe to toe with death, and you gotta be one hell of a tapdancer to outrun him.
bambino cop like you oughta show respect to those of us who's hung in long enough to know what coppin' was like back when gravity was the only law.'

'with all due respect' she said, and then she showed him exactly the respect he was due: 'i wouldn't pull you from a burning car. this planet will be better off the minute each and every one of your contemporaries is a photo in a frame, a vague memory and nothing more. '

'dogs like us are working the graveyardshift at the exit door to life itself. and the life expectancy on us ain't long – i've survived those odds so far, detective. do i make myself *clear*?'

calhoun exhaled and a rotted tooth fell out of his mouth. he stepped towards rex and shattered the tooth against the floorboards with the tread of his 12 tonne boot.

rex fell back off the veranda and tumbleweeded into the yard. he loomed over her casting, a long, fat shadow.

'i've learned too much here, haven't i?' scrambling to her feet, sprinting towards her cruiser.

'just like that dead negro you loved so much.' calhoun said,

a wave of biblical anger rose up in kim rex with such force she felt as though the whole reason she got born was just so she could feel this.

she spun around on both heels. she faced the crime scene. she pulled her gun from her holster, tried to steady her trembling hand and squeezed the trigger.
a flame spat from the end, a cylinder left the muzzle.
commissioner calhoun blew back against the door, gripped his bleeding head in agony, slid to the floor.

she'd missed. but she'd blown his ear clean off. a torrent of blood and earwax shot from the wound like a soda stream. his huge porky head deflated.

her eyes narrowed. the barrel of her gun glistened in the evening light.

an engine roared behind her. the photographer leapt from a car, snapping pictures wildly, kodak film cannisters falling to the floor. he wields this lens that's about 40 metres long. 'hey what the hell's going on here? is that the corpse? my god! my god!'

rex smiles at him says 'i'll be right back!' (a lie) darts into her car. kickstarts the engine. screaming tires as she peels off, heavy panting into light traffic.

you wake up into another dream, empty the rat trap, suck the poison off your fingers. it tastes like lemongrass. the chinese make everything. and everything the chinese make they make chinese. passing through the tunnels of your apartment – a pre-fab four chinz job, geriatric ward wallpaper peeling like skin at the corners, LCD screens on standby glow green like lizard eyes. is it looking in or looking out? – fuck, i know dogs that got it better than this. you got a slotomatic coffee faucet in sleek chrome where the kitchenette used to be, works on a retina scanner: scans your eyes and works out how much caffeine you need and spurts ambition into a cup … today? two shots. tomorrow: the world.

 shallow breaths and deep aches, bones are sore and nipples are vibrating like tiny flesh washing machines.

fold back the venetian double blinds, metal slats bounce neon sunlight into the room, and you catch your body reflected in the window pane …

you are flesh on the bone,

lots of it,

your nakedness sits awkwardly on your skeleton.

slathered across it and oodling off of it

you are an apparatus of pumping

and piping,

blood tunnels, valves, food fat,

sacks of shit and piss,

intestines curling inside you

like a brown snake,

but

your skeleton waits inside all this,
patiently waits
for you to die.

somedays you catch your reflection and you think 'god i am hot stuff, i look good, man' …

today ain't that day.

caffeine brown greases the cogs, the computer whirs to life.
today we make sweet love to our sour existence.

i sit at the kitchenette counter – puke coloured formica (my
choice, not the the landlady's) and running a prickle point up my
arm and across the round part of my shoulder. i make a tough
guy face in case anyone's watching thru the lizard eye, and i
drive the steel triangle in, into my flesh. swirl it around like i'm
giving a gentle stir to some soup, the hole widens like porno, and
out if pops: a little white ball of congealed pus, dangling by a
thread of unwound cartilage. my indifference on a string. i sever
the pus ball, flick it like a spitball to the ceiling, and sew myself
fucking shut. washing blood off my hands, look at the scar – a
neat sew job, with cartilage for thread. even got it to do a nifty
zig zag motion n all.

i put on my dress-down attire cause i'm between bosses at the
moment.

i smirk back at the new pus ball clinging, blood spattered to the
ceiling,

a constellation of 200 or 300 just like it. this is my system for
counting the days …

300 days since the infestation began.

i exit my pre-fab. i exit my apartment.

careful not to hit myself in the ass with the door.

i go over to the Hospital. top doctors. it's the place where george clooney got his brain tumor removed. they got a picture of him framed above the reception, like an italian restaurant 'look who ate here!' kinda snap. him in a green gown, eyes glazed over, scalped, big frigging cleave in his pretty-boy head. the star of *ER* indeed.

signage says *psych ward* is on level 3. i take the stairs.

BUCKSHOT

loaded buckshot into the cylinder,

tied barn twine to the big toe on one foot, fed it thru the
fingerguard of the shotgun,

wrapped it round the trigger, and double knotted it to be sure.

huddled up on a hay bale

all fetus like

goodbye today and hello tomorrow,

wrap my mouth around both barrels

close my eyes

now just gotta step forward with one leg

like i'm walking off into space

(O)

some people say you can measure inflation by the price of a mars bar. other people say they can no longer afford a mars bar.

A DREAM SHE HAD

she turns to me and she says 'i had a beautiful dream last night. i dreamed a movie'

her coffee cup in her hand, pack of cigarettes on the table.

and to me she looked like she was in a movie

she dreamed

about rubber on tarmac, a street lined with evenly spaced trees, she dreamed of impossible beauties, uplit and in danger.

she dreamed in black and white, there may have been subtitles, it may have been silent.

does it matter? dreams like movies are mostly a visual medium.

dreams like movies are approx 90 mins long.

she says 'how can i respect a man who pretends to be somebody else for a living.'

she says

'i know you don't think of yourself as an actor. you think of yourself as a artist. … but you are *all* pretend and i've never once seen you *reveal yourself.*'

'that's a good point' i said. 'i guess i'll try and … *bare* that in mind.

'you spelled bear wrong' she said.

i blinked quizzical

'you gotta remember to keep the grizzly bear. up here.' and then she tapped the side of head. her temple.

by now the cigarette smoke was billowing, or clouding, billowing. around her hair. her beehive. around the 60s.

we're on a balcony.

beneath us: roaring fires as baby petrol gangs crawl the angry
streets, chimneys made from buildings and crematoriums at our
feet. they chant a rage magnificent, and feed our beautiful people
into the flames. to these pissed off mutant babies our world is
a joke and a playground – street signs become hockey sticks,
upturned cars become trampolines, this boulevard a bowling
alley, a sandpit made of ash. and with lassos they scale the
walls, they ski up mountains made of glass. the city quakes as it
knows it is a goner, it parts its lips and scratches its wrist, high
rises belch, a panoramic restaurant spins off its axis, fire escapes
contort, balconies buckle, antennas fold like jackknives. a model
on a billboard gets a flaming phone box to her pretty winking
eye. sirens scream, sirens scream and radios blare the test signal,
across from us there's another balcony, on another building. a
balcony that holds two other people: twins stapling their hands
together.
together they take the leap, eyes closed. radios blare the test
signal.
the ground beneath it all begins to tremble, the ground begins
to buck, before long the ground is cumming. a blinding
flare! impossible heat! eyes closed, still blinded, scorched by
purity. a huge flame from the molten core of the centre of the
earth.
and you grip my arm. 'that's no camera flash, friend. but you can
smile if you wanna.'
the babies look up in wonder as the sky drips icky white.

the twins return as angels,
the rubble takes a sigh,
 the fires recede politely.
the city clears its throat.

the rustle of darkness.

the hum of hot wires …

we click our fingers and
off goes the show.

was at a bar the other night. staring down into my 4th beer.
of the night. not of ever.

when i'm alone i like to sit up at the bar ... that way you're not
staring at an empty chair.

adam came in and sat on the barstool next to mine. yes, *that*
adam.

i didn't recognize him at first ... cause he had his clothes on
overtop his figleaf. and he was looking pretty good for his age. i
asked him his name, he told me, i said 'adam who?', he said 'just
adam', i said 'what ... like ... as in ...'

he sighed. gently irritated to be explaining this for the 1,000,000,
000,000,000,000,000,000,000,000,000,000,000,000,000,
000,000,000,000,000,000,000,000,000,000,000,000,000,000,000,
000,000,000,000,000,000,000,000,000,000,000,000,000,000,000,
000,000,000,000,000,000,000,000,000,000,000,000,000,000,000,
000,000,000,000,000,000,000,000,000,000,000,000,000,000,000
,000,000,000,000,000,000,000,000,000,000,000,000,000,000,00
0,000,000,000,000,000,000,000,000,000,000,000,000,000,000,00
0,000,000,000,000,000,000,000,000,000,000,000,000,000,000,00
0,000,000,000,000,000,000,000,000,000,000,000,000,000,000,00
0,000,000,000,000,000,000,000,000,000,000,000,000,000,000,00
0,000,000,000,000,000,000,000,000,000,000,000,000,000,000,00
0,000,000,000, 000,000,000,000,000,000,000,000,000,000,000,00
0,000,000,000,000,000, 000,000,000,000,000,000,000,000,000,00
0,000,000,000,000,000,000, 000,000,000,000,000,000,000,000,00
0,000,000,000,000,000,000,000,000, 000,000,000,000,000,000,00
0,000,000,000,000,000,000,000,000,000,000, 000,000,000,00
0,000,000,000,000,000,000,000,000,000,000,000,000,000, 000,00
0,000,000,000,000,000,000,000,000,000,000,000,000,000,000,000
, 000,000,000,000,000,000,000,000,000,000,000,000,000,000,000,
000,000, 000,000,000,000,000,000,000,000,000,000,000,000,000,
000,000,000,000, 000,000,000,000,000,000,000,000,000,000,000,
000,000,000,000,000,000, 000,000,000,000,000,000,000,000,000,
000,000,000,000,000,000,000,000, 000,000,000,000,000,000,000,
000,000,000,000,000,000,000,000,000,000, 000,000,000,000,000,
000,000,000,000,000,000,000,000,000,000,000,000, 000,000,000,

000,000,000,000,000,000,000,000,000,000,000,000,000,000, 000,
000,000,000,000,000,000,000,000,000,000,000,000,000,000,000,0
00, 000,000,000,000,000,000,000,000,000,000,000,000,000,0
00,000,000, 000,000,000,000,000,000,000,000,000,000,000,0
00,000,000,000,000, 000,000,000,000,000,000,000,000,000,000,0
00,000,000,000,000,000,000, 000,000,000,000,000,000,000,000,0
00,000,000,000,000,000,000,th

time.

'it wasn't so bad before the bible came out' he said. 'before that piece of shit nobody had ever heard of me, but now i gotta explain myself constantly'

i sipped my beer and tried not to be starstruck.

he showed me his drivers license and sure enough = just adam.

i bought him a beer. it seemed like the right thing to do. besides, it was about time for me to have another one anyhow. the beers came and we tugged on them.

'so ... adam ... uh ...' i said, after a big big while. 'what do'ya think about all this gender is a construct stuff?'

'loada bollox'

i tugged on my beer a little more. ... tried to soften him up.

'what about how gender is a sliding scale?'

'not for me it ain't'

hmm, i thought, men of certain age, men of a certain age.

'howsabout the notion that uh,,, gender is performed?'

'dogshit straight outta rover's ass'

we both tugged at our beers.

'how about ... fixed genders are a thing of the past? something we're evolving out of?'

adam paused for a long time and then said 'you could be onto something with that. i don't know very much about the future.'

now there was something we had in common. we both tugged on our beers some more. i had just written a poem about how disgusted i am by my own birth cause it proves my mom once did it.

adam listened pretty intently then said ... 'how many guys ever fucked your mother? about 1/2 dozen? a dozen? two dozen at most? ... that's nothing. the whole species makes it with mine.'

'how so?'

'i'm the first man. i ain't got no mother except mother nature …
you, me, n all the men in between done fucked her pretty good.'
'well adam, i guess i never thought too-too much about who
your parents is.'
'The Father is my father, and The Mother is my mother … &
that's why the world is so fucked up. they been divorced since
forever.'
adam ordered a round of beers and we tugged on them. i asked
again about the gender thing.
'you really think it's a performance?' he raged. 'do i look like an
actor?'
he didn't look like any particular actor so i said so. he told me
i looked like the product of a one night stand between steve
buscemi and tilda swinton … and that i'd come out looking not
quite as ugly as him but not nearly as beautiful as her.
i shot back: 'give me time!'
adam laughed a lot. like a drain. to a guy adam's age that's a hell
of a thing for a 30 year old to say.
'time?' he thundered 'you don't know squat about time,
sunshine. i've had naps longer than your life.'

they called time at the bar.

adam invited me back to his place. said he had a bottle of scotch
about 200 years old, bin waiting for an occasion to open it …
why not?
adam was pretty swift with a smartphone – no slouch for an
old geezer. dialled in an uber pretty sharpish. told me the
smartphone technology didn't phase him – they had the same
thing in ancient egypt, he said, before the martians totalled the
place, of course. the car came, we got in.
'if you wait long enough everything comes back round'
'is that so?' i said as we pulled out into traffic.
& with a twinkle in his eye he said it again …
'if you wait long enough everything comes back round'
'is that so?'
'if you wait long enough everything comes back round'
'is that so?'

– we giggled
'if you wait long enough everything comes back round'
'is that so?'
'if you wait long enough everything comes back round'
'is that so?'
then he took a big pause …
before starting it up again. we had the same sense of humour.
'if you wait long enough everything comes back round'
'is that so?'
'if you wait long enough …'
– we did this all the way to peckham.

his apartment was just by queen's rd station. much smaller than
i'd expected.
he explained it was a friend's, he didn't really live there, said his
first home – the *garden* – had spoiled him for living anywhere
else, ye know? he said he was just watching this flat while the
friend was away, watering the plants and so forth.

i looked around. didn't see any plants.

we sat on the grotty futon. an energy saving bulb blazed limply
overhead.
adam poured some of the 200 year old scotch. it tasted like
turpentine to me, but i made the right noises. i'm a good date.
i brought up the gender thing one more time. i had a hunch that
if i could just get him drunk enough …
he stood up in a rage, dropped his jeans and boxers, unzipped
his fig leaf … and there, beneath a wispy threadbare tuft of pubic
hair that'd been grey since 5000BC. was an apologetically small
pecker, uncut, shrivelled like dried fruit, not so much trouser
snake as trouser dew worm.
he pointed at the thing with drunk guy swagger: 'does THIS
looks like a SLIDING SCALE to YOU?'
'well' i said.

he drunkenly fumbled with his jeans, bent over yanking at 'em, to get 'em back on. it was then that i saw he had skidmarks in his figleaf.

he apologized about that, 'eve used to take care of that for me … not sure how, bleach i guess'

he sat down, embarrassed.

'just wipe more, man'

'i wipe until i bleed & still i get these skidmarks.'

he drained his scotch glass. i drained mine.

'you think with my infinite prison sentence on this planet i haven't had time to solve the puzzles of existence that *can* be solved? somethings are designed to stump mankind forever … brown streaks in the underwear is one of them things!'

'i just wear boxers' i said, which is the truth of the matter.

'i need more support than that'

he poured us another glass each, very long looking doubles.

'i thought you and eve were naked' i said, 'when i seen pics of you two … when you was an item, i mean …'

he got misty eye'd explaining they'd been together and apart countless times. 'sure the first time had ended badly – damnation of the entire species n all … but they kept coming back to one another. he fought back tears, said he was basically sure that she was The One.'

i sipped my scotch. he blew his nose into the sleeve of his jacket, red face from crying.

okay, i thought, he's really softened up now … let's try this one more time …

'adam' i said 'ya know how you showed me your pecker as a way to prove your gender? well, ya see, that's kinda irrelevant. cause the way us youngsters got it figured, sex and gender are two separate things, that vary independently, so, while there's a strong correlation between peckers and being a man, it's by no means proof … there's a lotta women that have peckers, & a lotta men who do not …'

'yeah yeah' he said, mumbled something about they had a similar concept in the ottoman empire, 'before the martians put the kibosh on that of course.' he said, falling silent, losing his train of thought. thank gosh.

i whispered so as to not be too threatening as i blew his mind: 'and there's also folks who are neither man nor woman. and folks who are both man and woman. and some of 'em gots peckers and some of 'em don't.'

he took it all in. perhaps against his will. he closed one eye, did the drunk-sway, trying not to fall down despite already being sat down thing.

i figured that was the lesson part of the evening over ... tried to think up something, anything, to lighten the mood.

'uhh ... i know ... hey, adam ... i can't believe i didn't think of this the minute we met ... i have something that belongs to you. i've been carrying it my whole life, do you want it back ... ?'

he stared at me like he'd heard this once an hour his whole life. i tried to complete my joke but i couldn't ... because it was *stuck in my throat.*

as the evening tore on adam got belligerent. typical alcoholic – only fun for the first few drinks ... he starting belly-aching about immortality, saying it takes the stinger out of life if you can't die. kept apologizing for the shame you and me feel about our nakedness ... kept saying *way* more of the blame should be heaped on him, how guilt devoured eve's soul, how she was never the same after the fall from grace. then the next minute he'd be up dangling his pecker in my face proclaiming a love of alcohol saying how it's an elixir to numb the shame. then he'd say eve was an incorrigible flirt and how'd he know that's ALL that happened with the snake? what if she'd fed the serpent inside herself and dildo'd herself all the way to a burning goddamn bush?
'adam i think it might be time for bed' i said as he started a one man conga line.

'yeah, i agree. let's fuck.' he tumbled towards me, bashed his knee on the ikea coffee table, too drunk to notice. 'let's do it. you and me.'

'that's not what i meant' i said ...

and it wasn't what i meant ... but ... i did think, how many chances like this am i gonna get? i mean, we are ALL descended from him. it's the ultimate incest daddy-issues taboo 2, what if ron jeremy were your dad? moment.

so i took one for the species.

and i seized it:

i leaned forward, squeezed my eyes shut. and kissed him.

planted a big wet one on him, sloppy mouths sliding across eachother like boozy slugs.

he took me by the wrist and led me to the bedroom – a double mattress on the floor, a fish tank with algae scum and a couple dead fish floating in it, a map of the world with push pins marking travel destinations: goa, the camino, burning man festival, disneyland paris. there was a framed poster of the chat noir. 'that poster comes with every house' i thought, 'why frame it?'

adam was tumbling out of his jeans, flopping back on the mattress, apologizing but insisting that *he* would *not* be taking *his* shirt off – biblical self consciousness and all.

i pointed at the chat noir and asked if the fish in the tank had died outta fear. he didn't get it ...

i perched on the edge of the mattress, took a big drink of air.

i laid myself on top of him, we caressed and dry humped about forty humps. he invited me to de-robe, so i did. he complimented me on my hairless body, 'like a sphynx' he said, and tried to tell me how the martians architected the pyramids, as though we hadn't covered that twice already ... we made out some more, i nibbled his collarbones and kissed the front of his neck, and licked sweat off his, well, HIS apple. he rolled me over and grazed my thighs with limp fingers – there's a place at the top of my pelvis where if i'm touched just right i get shivers. i did the same back to him and he made deep, long groaning sounds when i got it right. he touched me quite rough, like i was made of plastic or graphite or like he had more practice touching rubber body parts than real ones. he touched me like i didn't have feelings, like i was an object, and i know it sounds funny, but i was worried for my life, a fleeting flash of this must be how the mouse felt in lennie's hand.

we pushed our groins together but neither of us could get hard = whiskey dick'd.

so it was just flaccid sweat patch on flaccid sweat patch, germ farm to germ farm.

eventually our grinding rhythm slowed to nothing, the rhythm of defeat.
i rolled away from him, faced the wall. and he spooned me gentle from behind.
through the night, he stroked my lower back, cupped my buttocks, occasionally spreading my cheeks apart, he marveled at how hairless i am … 'even in there' he'd whisper.

we drifted in and out of sleep. the morning arrived. it brought sunbeams and hangovers.

adam told me he'd been with 1000s of guys over the years and that i was the best one yet. i knew he was lying … our attempt, had been quite the abortion, but it was sweet of him to lie. it showed he cared about me. it off-set the self-loathing that usually sets in the morning after. and i thought maybe this ain't bad practice … complimenting a one night stand, no matter how bad it'd gone. send them away with a little more confidence than they came to you with … who's it hurting?

over breakfast he apologized generically. it was clear he didn't remember any specific transgressions, but he'd awoken with that familiar feeling, the shame that comes with the knowledge that last night was *yet another* one of *them nights*.

adam scrambled some eggs. and sniffed some back bacon to determine the use-by date was a con. he turned stale bread into burnt toast. and drowned everything in ketchup for both of us.

i stood up to leave and a tear came to his eye. he thanked me for pushing him to think new thoughts last night. he admitted that a few times over the years – or maybe quite a few times every year – he'd had fleeting thoughts. little notions. creepy suspicions. hunches. that maybe. perhaps. he wasn't or isn't 100%, all the time, male.

he said that if he'd learned one thing in all his time on earth it was that the right answer usually turned out to be live and let live … he said that in his day they didn't have language for expressing the nuances of identity & that maybe there was a very dark part of him that wanted everyone to suffer the way he had. to suffer. to be imprisoned. he sobbed and pulled me close to him. he asked for forgiveness.

'and and and …' he cried 'being the First Man. is my entire identity. if i didn't have that … if i didn't have that … what would i have?'

i held his face against my torso. i clasped him to my pigeon chest.

he sobbed and wheezed and soaked my t-shirt right thru.

his breathing slowed eventually, his sob became a whimper.

i have this rib – the bottom rib – it juts out quite a bit.

he gripped it very gently, pincered it between two fingers.

'this' he said 'this rib … would make a helluva woman.'

i giggled.

'we've all got a little woman inside us, innit?' he said, and then he nibbled on my rib playfully, like he was pulling pork from the bone.

we went into the hall to make our goodbyes. he kept apologizing and thanking me.

then a look of pride rippled down his face, like he was about to give me an expensive xmas gift.

he slowly lifted up his shirt, to show me what he had been too shy to show me the night before …

he had heavy scarring up and down his torso, a zig zag pattern like the london tube map …

'i tried to remove … all … the female parts of me' he said 'but it didn't work. (whimper.) it didn't take the feelings away.'

'so you don't have *any* ribs?' i asked.

he smiled coyly, yellow teeth. i placed my palm on his torso, bang in the middle, nipples above and navel below. where the rib cage should be. i pushed in gently, felt fatty skin folds but no ribcage. i pushed harder, it gave like a waterballoon, i pushed some more, 6 or 8 inches deep into him now, i could feel organs and scraps of food in there, fluids sloshing around and a tumor or two that had failed to kill him. i pushed all the way in until … i felt his spine … i gripped his spine! '… no ribcage.' i said, making the awe face.

he pulled his shirt back down.

just then he excused himself real abruptly and dashed into the bathroom. to vomit.
maybe the bacon *was* off.

'uh' i said 'uh' knocking on the bathroom door. 'uh … i guess i'll let myself out'
i listened through the bathroom door. i listened to the sound of his hurling.

& then i did something quite shameful … i rifled through adam's coat pockets, found his wallet – not to steal money … i wanted his driver's license. as a souvenir. to prove it to people! who would believe me without it? – oyster card, pizza express vouchers, i heard the toilet flush, there it is QUICK, i stuffed it into my pocket and ninja-starred the wallet onto the table with the keys and telephone and the unopened mail.

i slipped out the door silently, and bolted down the hall.

my mind raced as i ran: now when people say 'you don't know me from adam' i can say 'yeah i do' ... and whip the license out. shame nobody has said that in 50 years ... but if adam's right, it'll come back around ... if you wait long enough everything comes back round.

i was so paranoid adam'd twig it missing & come after me that i sprinted the entire way back to my pad in lewisham. i crahed thru the door, out of breathe, full of adrenaline, hangover pounding, i slammed the door shut and locked it behind me, pulled the drivers license out of my pocket.

there it was ... adam.

adam ... justinawitz.

i rubbed the 2nd name on the laminate card. i rubbed my eyes. i shook my head like *cartoon double take noise*. i turned the card over. i held it up to the light.

it was the same card i'd seen last night only ...

only ...

last night he'd had his thumb over his last name.

adam justinawitz
D.O.B: 04/04/1948
place of issue: ilford

'every alcoholic has a trick for getting strangers to buy them drinks' friends said 'every broke boozer has a con'
'but you don't understand' i chirped 'you don't understand'
i told 'em about the fig leaf … 'so what?'
i told 'em about his ribs … they said 'marilyn manson had his ribs removed, that doesn't prove much'
'yeah' another said 'he prolly just wanted to suck his own dong.'
'maybe' i said, trying not to get emosh, *exhale exhale*
'what was his dong like?' they all wanted to know.
i pictured it … 'in truth it wasn't much of a dong … really more of a ding.'
we all laughed. and they passed the card around. they rode me about having, well, kinda, having made it with a dude older than velcro.
i swore i'd never drink again. so we ordered a few beers to celebrate that decision.

we googled the name adam justinawitz and found he'd been brought to england in his mother's belly, as part of the polish re-settlement act, 1947. she'd had a rough ride in ww2, come to england and been plonked in the norwhick park camp. adam had been raised there.

it wasn't quite as good as biblical adam, i supposed. but he was still a piece of history …

'ding' somebody said again. 'really more of a ding.'

recovering drg ppl gots chronic *boredom*. always gotta have a cig in they mouth, a coffeecup in they hand, always gotta be on the way somewhere or on the way back. they don't sit still good, and when they do sit still good they don't shut up good: *yeh, i jus bean to hell. joo wanna see the slideshoe? it wasn't as coo as i thought it was gon' be. ha-ha-ha-ha. thas a joke tho, don't laff. i juice gut back uh. moment ago or two maybe i dunno. you know what my mammary is like – out the widow. anywhy did you won see these pitchers or shall i juice describe it to ya? a pitcher's worth a 1000 words, i took about 1000 pitchers, uh this could take a vile. uh-huh-huh-huh. strap in … maybe get yourself a drank from the bar. o yeah you don't drunk, i forget. you don't lick to party. uhhh speedking of party i got these wild pills man i don't no, water they are. might be anti-depressors mang, wild stuff, you pop a bunch of 'em – or ye crush 'em up n snore 'em – and you no longer want to diet. uh-huh-uh-huh-uh-huh-uh, … sounds like quite a drip. let me know if i can hike you up. huh huh huh either that or i'll be pulling ya down from a belt loop attached to the ceiling fan one of these days, am i right? uh huh huh. okay, sippycups, i'll shit you later.*

phantom tongue twisted, split in half right down the centre line by a specially bladed knife to make a two pronged licking machine just like a lizards. man is making himself into a lizard and he's up there on a tv soundstage being grilled by an every-woman empathy drone who spent 4 hours in makeup, whose hair stays still even when she turns her head. he's explaining himself to the world: her, me, you, the studio audience who entered a raffle for tickets and every pair of eyes that's home at 3pm and within signal range of this satellite. scales etched into the skin canvassed across his frame, teeth filed to a point, contact lenses and a row of convex metal pucks running a dotted line down his spine, and he's on this show cause he's saving up for a detachable tail to complete the transformation. 'aren't you afraid that people will stare at you in restaurants?' the question asker sucks in air through her surgically enhanced lips and wets her regulation tongue with the only water brand she's contractually allowed to sip and it's a good thing they were forthcoming with a sponsorship deal last season or she'd've died of thirst. man is making himself into a lizard, peeling back to where we all came from, that animal, that instinct, that cold blooded shield sheathed intrinsic that gave us all the right to say 'i dunno why i do what i do, but damn if it don't feel good' and i gotta admit yes i gotta … i know what old split tongue means: cause if the technology exists to make us all different then why use it to make us all the same? and question queen's forehead would be sweaty if it could still perspire. and her brain instructs her face to paint a picture of understated something or other but it's locked between expressions by sheets of rupturing botox … and if it weren't for the camera angles and station break announcements would you know which one of these is supposed to be the freak? cause i'd rather be ridiculed for being a good version of me than a sloppy botch job of somebody else. 'some of these procedures are irreversible, you do know that, doncha dear?'

& the next guest discusses this week's book club recommended reading: chicken soup for the holocaust deniers soul. *ooo-weee! gotta get myself to the li-bra-ry!*

next up is fashion coroner, what is in and what is out? she uses
a ouija board to dial up audrey hepburn's corpse and wheel it
into the studio. and it offers its 2 cents – which if ya factor in
inflation, is like, i mean, in audrey hepburn's day 2 cents could
buy you a house. audrey says you can wear a short skirt with
a turtle neck or a long skirt with a low cut top. or a turtle dove
with a lo-res jpeg of a boot. but you cannot wear a turtle head …
and a high-necked noose.

but ya shit yerself when ya hang.

we flick the flicker goodnight.

 the transmission is off air and

we turn to each other and say

'isn't the world a crazy place?'

& for all we know there's a tv news anchor loading a pistol into
his mouth in the dressing room of a soundstage, for all we know
someone is loading a pistol into their mouth in this theatre as
we speak. (it could be me, i gotta very big mouth, there's plenty
of room for a pistol … and all these words.) my eyes close just
long enough for dust to settle on the lids. we are writhing naked
bodies, dithering on the storm. we are machines that go squish
in the dark. contraptions dismantling ourselves. in sleep we force
ourselves to change. we perform the inner autopsy, looking for
signs of infection, signs of abuse, signs of life. any signs at all …
like … how many miles til the next exit? … we take the off-
ramp.

     'isn't the world a crazy place?' you say again,

in the morning & i say

   …y e a h , i t 's t h e *o n l y* p l a c e :
a l l t h e c r a z y p l a c e s a n d a l l t h e n o t c r a z y
p l a c e s …
s m u s h e d t o g e t h e r …
i t 's a l l t h e p l a c e s a t o n c e , t h e w o r l d i s
t h e w o r l d.

ur gone

now we read passages
of the only good poet
to each other
across the death divide

ur gone

you guide my hand
to the pen,
to the straight razor,
to the gay razor,
but never to my throat

ur gone

stay gone

dead.

WE'RE GONNA NEED A BIGGER AMP

my guitar is louder
than the voices in your head

but i am on the lookout
for an even bigger amp

cause my guitar is not as loud
as the voices in my head.

JAZZ STAINS

i am learning the saxophone

my neighbours are learning they hate the saxophone

they are faster learners than i am

i play it so loud

it leaves jazz stains allover the room

i think i just killed the cat

with a 115 db B flat

in an apartment the same square footage

as your twat

the neighbours are pounding and screaming

the pounding makes an ok metronome

but the screaming is not a very *jazz* vocal

i bet pharoah sanders never had this problem

i bet pharoah sanders never lived in lewisham

next to a bunch of cretins

who are annoyed i'm drowning out their x box.

SOUL GUN

2005,
buffalo, new york

… meanwhile at the precinct:

'DON'T LEAVE TOWN!'
a suspect has their face smashed off a tin table top
blood trickles out of their nose
forming a ginger goatee.

the detective swaggers out of the interview room.
he swaggers into the lunchroom.
he swaggers up to the drip coffee machine and drinks straight
from a glass beaker.
his germs are transferred onto the glass!
they don't teach humility at the police academy.

'that ain't hygenic' says the cleanest cut copper on the force.

the television in the corner of the room blares reruns of the
weather channel.
the detective pulls a six shooter from his belt and fires it at the tv.
the screen explodes showering the room in plate glass, chunks
of cathode ray and tiny vapors of an unknown gas which may or
may not have played subtle havoc on the psyches of everyone
assembled.

'still using that antique?' says the lizard-skinned latino cop in the
corner. a spider crawls out from under his grease pit hairdo and
drops dead from the stench of him. the reek of last night's rim
jobs comes wafting toxic from his emaciated pervert lips.

'what of it?' the detective grumbles.

'dig this' says the lizard, producing a futuristic looking weapon. a pistol made of neon glass. adjustable guage, from 22 to 38, vari focal scope with zoom lens, fingerprint safety lock, glows in the dark, gps tracking, usb port, doubles as an mp3 player, custom magazine sizes, unlimited reload, telescopic silencer that extends up to two metres for stealth killing at a distance 'and dig this ...' the lizard brags 'this gun takes a photograph in tandem with firing the bullet. i got a photo of the look on every face i ever blew away, right as i did so ...'

'that's nothing' she lays down a slimy pistol onto the table. not only wet and scaled, the thing appears to be moving ... this ain't just *cloaked* in snake skin friends. this gun is *alive*. and the pistol hissed through gritted teeth and slithered around on the tabletop.
'fashioned from organic matter? somehow carved from the body of a snake?' they asked.
'no, naturally occurring. i tamed her on a trip thru the amazon. needs a human to operate her. she chooses a human bride. a master.'
kim rex and the snake gun then tongue kissed.

'how's your living love gun good for anything else that my pocket rocket ain't?'

just then an expendable character walked in on the scene. picture somebody totally nondescript. no definable features. somebody deemed Not Distracting Enough ... to be an extra. a man with blank paper for a face! that's who walks through the door. pow she fires her living pistol. there appears to be no contact – nothing leaves the gun. but the TARGET, he knows he's been hit. he looks down at his chest in terror, he's paralysed on the spot. starts whimpering like an infant, tears streaming his cheeks, lady cop still holds the gun outstretched. the gun barrel yawns open, flexing a beautiful jaw.

the victim grips his chest now and *noises noises* as a green gas
passes painful thru his ribcage, through his skin, through his
shirt. corroding each layer, leaving a toxic stain as it goes. inky
purple/black and the acrid smell of burnt tar.
this bubble of dark gas now floats in front of him
and he looks at it ... and he knows exactly what it is.
the gun barrel strains its jaws even wider as the gas ball drifts
towards it.
& gets sucked in ...
'what is happening?'
the gas ball meets the tip of the gun, the gun swallows it in an
indulgent feline gulp. unghh.
the lips of the gun shrink down again and her hole seals over
with a dainty belch.

all the other cops stand agape in disbelief.

including the featureless man whose chest is now a cindering tar
pit.
lady cop held court like a defence lawyer in the final throws
'gentlemen ... his soul!! sentencing him to a fate far worse than
death.'
the snake's skin glistened extra silky now. in kim's hand the
pistol began to throb, affectionate like a purring cat.
the victim dropped like a half tonne of bricks. crumpled to the
floor. smoke spiralled off him.

and the whole precinct erupted in a round of applause. kim rex
had done it again.

officer chuck delaney was there too that day, skulking in the
corner. and when kim rex got to the climax of her impressive
rendition the cock of delaney was growing out of him like a
corinthian column. it shattered the lunchroom wall! breeze
blocks crumbled like broken cookies as this architectural wonder
came piledriving forth from the poor guys jockey shorts! with
this corinthian column jutting out from him, delaney became
the laughing stock of the lunch room, and had no choice but to

go and lie down on the steps of city hall so his cock could stand amongst the other corinthian columns. he lay there the whole afternoon, until the sun started to set, with tourists and lawyers bustling by, wedding photos being taken. birds shitting allover him. delaney pictured kim rex firing that snake of a gun over and over again, each time picturing detective rex in a racier and racier outfit until such time as she was wearing only a badge! he climaxed hard and true, his sunburned corinthian column erupting at city hall like a domestic terrorist incident and raining thick globules of spunk junk down on the wedding couples like mushroom scented confetti.

this cock of delaney's sure had a way of getting him into tricky wickets. he was the only boy in his boyscouts batallion whose erections were proportional to the attraction that inspired them.

one time he apprehended a suspect by impaling him on the end of his erection. he was doing a ride along with an older cop, the two had come across a cat burglar who was about to get away, so delaney simply focussed real hard on one of his favourite masturbatory fantasies (the one in which the sorority girls are having the pillow fight and the pillows break open and feathers are flying everywhere and before you know it: cunnilingus!) that's all delaney had to think of (cunnilingus pillow fight) and whoosh … his cock like a harpoon, pinned the cat burglar to the brick of the alley way. the cat survived thankfully and was returned to its owner.

delaney got a commendation, his photo in the monthly round robin xerox and a fucking time piece or something. what time is it? time to get back to the story.

the irony of him bringing this rifle length pork pistol of his to the gun contest was lost on poor sweet, officer chuck, but is *not* lost on you, i suspect.

& just then:

a mouth on two squat legs came barrelling into the police station lunch room.

'walker, dupree, lorenzo, farenghelli, steele, croyzer, shampooj, kelly, geraldo, finkley, ambraham-kinney, fong, pupo, lau, charland, meuller, davis, cassidy, rollo, braxton, antonarovia, what the fuck are you all doing on your asses? i don't pay you to crack wise from the cracks in yer cornholes, i pay you to crack cases. there's murders that need solving, we got dumpsters full of body parts in this district, our local child prostitution industry has got more rings than a bigamists finger, are you waiting for a pay rise? are you striking? get outta my fucking sight. if i look like a bad guy to you you aren't spending enough time on the beat.'

there was a moan of complaint and somebody blamed confusion around the rotational system of who partnered with who. the mouth shot off again:

'arright break it up felines n fellas enough fuck muffin around. old guard ya got new recruits, the 411 from the big brass upstairs. i don't wanna hear no bellyache-ing or tear-jerking, we got people dying by the dozens out there and we don't know why. bring me answers, bring me evidence, file any complaints and queries direct into the in-tray i keep up your beloveds shite chute. you're working with partners from now on, no exceptions, no shirts no shoes no sunday service. get the fuck outta my sight.'

detective kim rex had been assigned a fresh faced boy partner, who she'd nicknamed angel breath.
he followed her down to the car lot and they piled into the cruiser.
'you sure you don't mind me tagging?'
she hadn't had a partner since grover white. grover white was an older cop that had taken kim under his wing. grover used to say 'well ...' and everybody liked him for that.

besides saying 'well …' there wasn't much to grover's character. maybe that was his secret to being such a good detective. that and unfaltering commitment. let me give you an example that just happens to be pertinent at this point in the story.

grover had been investigating this as yet unnamed criminal that kim rex would eventually travel to hell to apprehend. that's just one of many ways in which kim would walk in grover's footsteps. grover kicked down the door on the day they knew they'd got their man, charged into the room. their man knew he was facing forever and a day if not the chair so blew his face off with a shotgun. grover didn't miss a triplet … he shook off the gore like a wet dog getting outta the bathtub, raised his glock to his temple said 'don't think that's nuff to stop me comin' after you' and pulled the fucking trigger.

that was in april of '99. kim was the only one still holding a significant candle.

'he ain't ever come back' they used to say.

'yet' kim would say.

my soul won't rest til this thing is finished. kim's head said.

probably not the right time to traumatise poor angel face with that story. she started the engine and they peeled out.

'why wouldn't i want you along? because i'm a loose cannon? because i usually work alone? one who's truly secure in their individuality has nothing to fear from coupling and collaboration. it doesn't make me any less me to have you riding in the passenger seat.'

they stopped at a traffic light. the city looked most broken at night.

'i don't go in for that lone ranger shit. life is about connection to other people and the strongest willed among us can too oft forget that. what a male fantasy that is. to be an island. to *build* an island, to escape the rest of humanity. troubling and fetid as we *people* tend to be.'

she pulled a pregnancy test out from under her skirt. it was negative.

i been lucky so far in this life she thought *or maybe i'm infertile.*
she wound down a window and dropped the pregnancy test out.

' i may play a good tough guy down at the station, angel face, but don't be fooled. i don't harbour the desires of my father's generation. if i ever found riches it'd be community community community. you know? i don't need for much, not as far as material possession goes. i love my work and i still have my health and i barely ever see my apartment ... who would it benefit for my apartment to be bigger? greed breeds more greed. and i don't wanna be a part of that cycle.'

they sped on and on, him in silence thinking about what she said. her smiling wide, just happy to be alive. happy that grover white was still alive too. in her memories at least.

'why did you get into copping?' *angel breath* asked.
kim exhaled. 'you heard about true love? well, true hate works much the same way.'
'how bout you angel breath?' she asked, before he could prize her for clarification on whatever the hell it was that just came out of her mouth.
'how does a stud muffin like me get angel breath?' he thought to himself ... 'eating out angels i suppose.'

they stopped at a red light. the city was tar black behind it.
the light changed. the cop car peeled off down a side road.

'angel breath? please hold.' rex said, shushing him before he'd begun.

rex had spotted a dark figure ducking into the doorway of haberdashery.

the figure was acting furtive in a security camera blindspot. the figure stepped out of the blindspot and into the streetlight. it was a pregnant woman. bump n all.

rex slowed the car quickly and jumped out. she pulled a switchblade from her boot. she rushed after the pregnant lady, spun her around and muscled her into the doorway of a cantonese laundromat.

just my peking luck! thought the pregnant lady, *getting cornered with nowhere to run.*

the pregnant woman's eyes widened as detective kim rex plunged her knife direct into the pregnancy bump.

a cloud of white powder puffed from the gash. rex held the fake woman's eye contact in a deathstare as she licked the knife ...
CRACK COCAINE: just like she knew it would be!

angel breath radio'd for backup, charland & lorenzo pulled up, booked the perp, 'now that's what i call a crack baby' lorenzo said. charland said 'that's funny' but didn't actually laugh.

the crack started to immediately take hold. don't believe what your friends say about
crack being harmless. it is more than a gateway drug.

rex ambled jittery around the laundromat, fed coins into a tumbledryer for no reason. what a waste of money! after a few minutes another woman sauntered in, eyes darting furtively ... exactly like the first: pregnancy bump, gangland scar on the back of the hand. rex pulled her knife and the woman freaked, ran out of the laundromat, rex clattered through the door after her, chased her two blocks down. kicked her to the floor with a heavy boot, flipped the drug mule over and drove her knife straight down into the fake pregnancy bump ...

amneotic fluids gushed out onto the road, water broke allover the place, the uteral lining and bloodclots exploded, soaking a nearby taxi rank like someone let off a soviet firecracker filled with borscht.

'well you can't win 'em all.' rex said. wiping the fetus from the blade.

the mother doubled over in pain, sobbing.

rex looked down at the fetus. it looked up at her, glassy eyes like marbles in a deathstare. rosy pink cheeks like a funfair clown. tiny mouth in perfect finger suckling pout.
wearing a fabric blanket like a shawl. no fingernails – just the outlines of 'em carved into the plastic.
wait a mo, rex thought, lifting the blanket off the babies groin. finding no genitals at all, just a smooth plate. not even a hole to piss thru.
wait a mo mo minute ... this is a fucking doll.
she licked the blade again. opium this time.
a plastic baby doll filled with opium ...
damn chinese, damn russians.
rex squelched around in the liquids. she squelched around on the road. she picked up a bloodclot and popped it into her mouth.
it was borscht alright.
why such an elaborate and messy disguise ... ? why smuggle the drugs inside a plastic baby doll, inside a bowl of soup rigged with firecrackers, inside a fake baby bump strapped to a drug mule? it's almost like they expected to get caught. like they *wanted* to get caught.

rex swung around to quiz the suspect mother but she'd fled.

rex ran back to the laundromat. angel breath was pacing nervously by the cruiser 'i didn't know where you went!' he said. *fat load of good he was ...*

the laundromat door swung creaky on rusty hinges. traffic whined outside.

rex went into the laundromat and angel breath followed. she traipsed bloodclots and amneotic fluids allover the laundromat floor as she walked. splayed out on the tiles was a *third* fake pregnant drug mule. angel breath had shot her with a sleeping-dart, and was waiting for further instructions from rex. *maybe he wasn't so useless afterall* ... this one was unconscious alright, but her feet were kicking and she was whimpering softly. dreaming of long walks with master, perhaps. dreaming of being let off the leash to run free. she grit her teeth, dreaming of frisbee. rex knelt above the unconscious drug mule and stroked her hair. 'there there' she said 'that's a good boy. heel. heel.' rex whispered soft into the woman's ear, and in this way crawled into the woman's mind. once inside she threw frisbees for the woman, taught the woman to roll over. and allowed the woman to hump her leg a bit. rex's legs were much like rest of her: awful humpable! especially in a dream. she fed the woman liver pate, even smearing it on intimate parts of herself for the dog/woman to lick it off ... intimate parts such as the nape of her neck, the insides of her elbows and the tops of her knees. slurp slurp slurp went the dog lady, 'you can be happy like this forever' rex said to the dog/woman 'you can be happy like this forever if you turn your back on crime'. 'woof' said the woman, meaning okay that's a deal. and when the contract was all drawn up and rex felt she had the dog/woman's solemn promise to turn her back on crime ... she exited the woman's mind and emerged back out into the laundromat.

in the woman's mind she was slurping peanut butter from a jar of jiffy with her dog tongue but here in the laundromat she was lying on cold tiles, wagging her dry tongue across the nothing in front of her face.

rex held the woman close. *drug mules* she reasoned *are not real bad guys*. this motherf-er posing as a mother-to-be probably was a real life mother with a real mouth to feed. this was no kingpin, this was a street pawn, being used.

but so much of this case just didn't add up ... and that kind of thing bothered detective kim rex, which is partially what made her such a good detective.

she scanned the room for more clues but could see none. just the horrid scene in the street outside: the fake baby and the firework of fake lady innards. where did that exploding mother *go*?

just one more mystery lost to the night.

kim rex patted the rehabilitated dog woman on the head and stepped up to the laundromat counter and rang the bell for service.

an ancient cantonese man emerged from the backroom. he saw the mess of bloodclots and dog drool and amniotic fluids and swore in a language detective kim rex could not understand.
he said:
puk gai
ham gaa caan
tsat
lan
gau
diu
hai

walked into a public restroom.
not to take a rest, to take a shit.
coming out of the only stall – an
old-old-old-old man.
skin decomposing
though he's still alive,
hair like frayed nautical rope.
and he's shaking all diseased
as he pumps the handwash
and i'm thinking
with all we've achieved
why do i still have to step
into
a cloud of this man's ass dust
in order to undergo the …
waste disposal routine
that my body demands
almost daily
(daily if i'm remembering bran)
we can put men on the moon
or at least fake it n fool the world
and i am still sitting,
in his stench,
with zero doubt
what he had for lunch.
somebody wears a glove
to prepare my sandwich
and yet i breathe
particles of that man's
cancered colon.
you can buy apples pre-sliced,
so you don't need to own a knife
and here i sit
in this guy's aroma
like it's a cloud of fancy cologne
and i'd like it to cling to me for the rest of the day.

a viewfinder of light receptors and pulp-skin magnets for
receiving, decoding and in the extreme, deceiving the brain, like
so many addicts before i had found something i loved more than
i loved myself, and i knew it was evil as i swallowed it down,
and i knew well it was evil as i swallowed it down and i thought
'well this is evil' as i sucked each evil down. sucked it up, back,
in. gently, rough, hard and gradual, a wrong doing right of
passage, a footstep in a cliche in a mistake made again and again
and again and again and again and again. rendered normal,
and again and again and again and again and again, rendered
insignificant and again and again and again and again and again
and again. by a world view, and i read it so it must be true, and
this feeling, this tradeoff this payload this worth-it-barely shake-
the-long-ass-day-off,

so delectable it's just gotta be devil designed.

cause like every addict before you you know what you are
giving up
everything
and that's a humdinger of a price-tag
 'everything' and he whispered 'you are everything to me' and
she knew that he was a liar,
that his pants were ... On Fire.

HOT SEX

we had hot sex against the radiator. not that you can have any other kind when the *radiator's* turned on.

i hi-fived him and my hand got really sore, like punching a brick wall.

'go easy when you touch me' he said 'i'm part metal'.

'you're what?' i said, shaking my sore hand, 'you're part metal?'

'yeah,' he said, 'i'm a son of a gun'.

'my dad's a 12 gauge shotgun.'

'well' i said, 'it's a miracle your mother survived the conception!'

AIRBAG IN MY CHEST

just one more accident crash matting into darwin's safety net.
held together by medical metal, the car crash didn't kill me,
and now me n the car are 24% the safe stuff. i got an airbag in
my chest in case it happens again. got a metal plate reinforcing
every flat surface of my sex made body. got a false tooth behind
every real one. got a wig of my own hair in a closet at home
cause my scalp got burned off when the engine exploded. got
an army of replacement fingers i bought offline and a pair of
shoes sandbagged to the floor, i screw my ankles in – left shoe
threaded, right shoe bayonet – cause the stumps i got lumped
with ain't wide enough to balance on. this chest of mine, this
torso is regulation issue. but the steering column that i'm
impaled on is not – it plunged through my middle upon impact
and cannot be removed for fear my heart would stop, so it's
sawed off flush as possible and the doctors melted skin to form a
tight seal. sometimes it throbs when the weather changes moods,
and on a clear night i can pick up radio signals. otherwise i feel
no pain and i'm glad to be alive. and for the smart asses amongst
you: no my sense of direction hasn't improved. i may have a
car's steering column lodged in my chest cavity but i still don't
know where the fuck i'm going.

the deathless walk amongst us,
bin alive forever,
five-ever, the really stubborn ones
are they inhuman? unhuman? human+?

realist says: death is the humanest thing about human beings
cynic says: death is the saving grace of human beings
cynic with a specific & unlikely speech impediment says: death
is the saving grave of human beings.
humanist says: shhhhh. don't speak ill of human beings.

shhhhh. don't speak ill of the dead …
well, that's ALL of us eventually.

we all get a clean rap sheet in the end

you can speak ill of the healthy
you can speak ill of the ill
& you can speak ill of the terminally ill

until they become the dead.

we all get a clean rap sheet in the end.

SADSACK SOUL

wandering thru the afterlife
killing time, while i wait for my transit home:
down an alley, i find a sadsack looking dufus. a soul down on his
heels. what's a matter, skip? can i foot the bill?
uh, i don't really identify as a soul he says. spirit maybe …
heyheyhey, you're a soul. you're a great soul. ya don't have
to start quoting otis redding or anything. ya just gotta be
comfortable in yourself. ya know, let it all hang out. or some of it
at least. let some of it hang out.
he relaxed and passed wind.
yeah maybe your right, man, thanks a lot, i feel a touch better.
and we two strolled back to the coast. both waiting for the ship
to come in.
sitting at the dock of the bayyy,
no ya don't have to do that, i said.
but i feel like it all of a sudden!
watching as the clouds roll awayyy,
well that's a shame. i said. maybe you were better off unhappy.
less annoying, less shrill that way.
wasting ti-i-i-i-ime.

one day pacman thinks to himself 'i wonder which is my better side?'

nearby a bumblebee crash landed onto the lips of a succulent flower. 'unghh' the bee thought. 'not again, i just can't do it again.' he went limp and slinked off, through the spring air. doing the flight path of shame, stinger between his legs.

ROCKET

i'm riding riptide on a rocket straight to your heart. straddling
n strapped in, burrowing into a hole ripped flesh in the face,
burning gasoline internal as this bullet travels your veins.
bottlenecking by a blood clot, skid marks on the body rot, thru
oceans of muscle and vistas of pain, slit cracks in an intestine
like a pipe sprung a sewage leak, shite bubbling like froth from
a boxers' split lip. cut the cord from the mains. my brain's been
dead for years.

and in the afterlife the punishment awaits: you spread peanut oil
on your asshole as ganesh lubes up his trunk. he says 'it'll take
more than your faith to save you from this.'

'do what you want to this body' you say 'but please set my soul
free.'

you can follow logic right down a big black hole or you can
follow me and take my hand and wait for the drugs to take hold

'don't protect me.' you beg 'don't protect me from anything …
especially myself.'

these words rot in your dying mouth.

WHAT DOES *INSEPARABLE* MEAN?

JUSTYOUTRYANDTEARUSAPART.

and i say 'i wanna eat you out' and you say 'why don't we order something instead?' and i say 'i'm not into bdsm, i'm no good at taking orders' and you say 'i'm not asking you to take the order, i'm asking you to pick up the phone' and i say 'have you ever had phone sex before? i can't imagine it being very sexy' and you say 'of course you think that, men are all about the visual' and I look away which is designed to prove you wrong but just ends up highlighting your point. and when i look back you're touching yourself or maybe you're not but that's what i'm picturing. 'what's come between us?' you say and i say 'proof that at least one of us had a good time' and you say 'premature ejaculation isn't funny' and i say 'is that because it's too soon?' and neither one of us laughs (but they do) and we stare awkwardness in the eye and we have to admit that we're drifting apart, like two pieces of drift wood that used to be one larger piece of drift wood, floating away from each other on a river that somehow has 2 currents. and so we're closer tonight that we've been in months even though tomorrow is one step closer to the end.

JUAN FOR THE MONEY

i was once hired to play elvis. the american rock n roll singer
and heartthrob. the king. and i was sent over to wales to train
with the premier welsh elvis impersonator of spanish extraction.
juan matrinez. stage name: juan for the money. and this is true.
he's in bridgend, wales and gigging most weekends. and the guy
can just channel the king. just opens his mouth and out pops the
king – singing voice, quotes from interviews. it's like the king is
in the room with you. and he doesn't look the spit of the king –
he's way more spanish than the king. and more welsh too, not
that you can see that part. but they both have the black quiff and
they both have killer dance moves and they both have these
piercing blue eyes. and i say to juan, i say 'what separates you
from all the hundreds of thousands of other elvis impersonators?'
and he says real humble like he says 'commitment'. what
commitment i say and he points at his eyes.
'these aren't natural' he says
'there's a guy over in tijuana or marakesh or some place and
he does this experimental surgery. he tattoos the eyeballs. rich
americans fly their daughters over there and gift them this
surgery cause it's illegal everywhere else – you want brown eyes
but yours are green? you want green eyes but yours are blue? no
problem.'
'so ... those aren't your natural eyes' i say 'you got 'em tattooed
to be the same colour as the king's?'
'yes i did' and he shows me a photo on his flip phone of him two
birthdays ago with brown eyes
now ... what i didn't tell juan (for the $) was that i myself had
never been a hundred percent otay with the colour of my own
eyes. they're this sort of murky blue-green hybrid and not like in
a cool david bowie way where one eye is one way and one eye
is the other way, it's like people are looking at my eyes going
'what colour are they? they're a mess.' and it has affected my
confidence since forever, you know, i used to avert eye contact
and i'd wear sunglasses a lot. even on overcast days. but what i
did say to juan was 'can you send me the details of that place ...
it's for research'
and he did.

and i went.
over to tijuana or marakesh or the yemen or wherever. you
know, used a travel agent.
and uhh … got my eyes sorted out. the doctor did a mock up on
his computer as part of the consultation:
here's how you'd look with green eyes, here's how you'd look
with blue eyes.
i wanted lime green but the doc talked me out of it. 'why you
want citrus vision?' he said. i went with the blue. and they lay
you out under anaesthetic and whatnot and a day or three later
you come round with these great big bandages on your eyes like
minority report and you pull those things off and wow … brand
new eyes, vision still twenty twenty, use this dropper twice a day
for 9 weeks, call me if there's any problems.
and there wasn't, thankfully.
but … it didn't quite fill the void, ya know? it looked good. i got
a lot of compliments and whatnot. 'wow chris, your eyes are
such a definite colour now' people would say.
and that felt good
but i started to realise. it started to dawn. on me. that i was
sort of. addicted now to the surgery. i started to look around at
different parts of my body and think. what would that be like
without freckles. what if this was smaller, more compact and that
was, bigger, more … expansive.
but this shit is expensive.
and surgery's not just for christmas.
so, i made my way back to tiujana or the bahamas or wherever
and i really went for it. ya know. i promised myself: this. is. it.
one big surgery to make all the changes you want to make and
then that's it. cold turkey, no more.
got a forehead reduction – got it down to a 3 and a 1/2 head …
any more would look unnatural, they warned.
i got a cheekbone enhancement, got the red tones in my skin
turned down,
got my eye bags taken from suitcase to fannypack.
and i got a vagina put into the palm of my hand.
they started doing 'em for death row inmates apparently, and
prison fatalities went down.
and presumably a handful of prisoners went down too. … on
their own palms. ha ha & arf arf.

and this hand job surgery took a lot longer than the eyeball
recoloration did – got this whole team of plastic surgeons doing
constructive surgery on the palm of my hand, trying to dig in a
nice cavity that's the right size and making realistic labia – nice
big set of majora, nice little set of minor and a clitoris just for
show. i got all the sizes and settings just like how i like and the
whole while i'm thinking 'this is the last purchase i will ever
make not gonna need to leave the house ever again. or buy
anybody a drink!'
and i get it home. my hand. and it's bliss.
for about a week.
and then i got that itch again, ya know.
so i'm on the phone to tijuana or texarkansas or whoever and
i'm like okay … one more … what else have ya got?
i got a pair of breasts. really big, like unnaturally big, like …
offensively big.
and not cause i'm particularly into that, but because it was the
same price no matter what size you wanted.
so i went for it, ya know, like at a buffet. it's the same price …
what else am i gonna do but eat til i puke?
so now i've got this vagina in my hand and these great big
balloons.
and i'm home every day fucking my hand and trying to shoot
jizz up onto my balloons.
and guess what? still not satisfied
ring ring to tijua-wherever
'any more plastic surgery and you'll be a mannequin' the doctor
says to me
'you want my western money or not?' i say
and i came back this time with an anus in my other palm, a hand
to replace the two i'd ruined annexing its way off my right wrist,
a pair of extra feet on my ass so i can jump while i'm sitting, a lip
darkening and a teeth whitening at the doctor's insistence and
a series of funnels and gutters that transfer my underarm sweat
into my urinary tract so all my smelly liquids come out the same
tube.
and after all that: they threw a fake pregnancy bump in just to
say thanks for the custom!
and now friends,
perfection was just a camera click away. the minute i rose from

this last frankenstein session i knew that life was smiling down on me, that i was a being more resplendent than nature ever intended and for the first time in my short little life i felt proud to be alive. proud to be a member of this species, rolling round this rolling rock far prettier and more efficient than god would ever have had me be, had he got his way.

'caught in a trap, can't walk in, can't walk out, cause i love ya too much baby'
that was juan for the money, serenading his fiance, in their kitchen when the phone rang.
he picked up the phone, slid it to his ear and ran his hands through his quiff.
it was me on the other end.
he told me all about how he'd met his match, and just got engaged: she was a marilyn monroe impersonator. she did a watershow on the docks of porthcawl, went by the name marilyn monrowboat.
'they say some like it hot …' he said 'but you know, chris, i think we all do.'
'you might be right about that juan, you might be right. hey … guess what?' i said.
then he covered the receiver and marilyn monroe boat said something.
'chris, it's late. can i call ya tomorrow?'
'uh huh'
and then juan put the phone down, and marilyn cradled him.
he sang into the crook of her neck … 'marlilyn marilyn marilyn marilyn, life is but a dream.'

YOU KNOW, YOU KNOW

you don't know what you don't know, but you know that you don't what you don't know. you know what you know, and what you know is all you know, and you know that, whether you know that you know that or not. one of the things that you don't know is what the rest of us knows. some of the things that you know are the things that i know but neither of us knows which is which. there is a lot that nobody knows. and nothing that everybody knows. you are an ignorant son of a bitch. and that bitch? she's the daughter of an asshole. and this ignorance doesn't skip generations. it is a constant from you all the way back to single cell sludge. so fuck you. and all of your ancestors.

i'm sorry, i've lost my train of thought … i'll have to say all that again.

(repeat speech ad nauseum)

DEAD MAN'S FACE

a tap on my shoulder. 'i'm sorry to do this to you' i turn. 'i'm so
so sorry to do this to you, but i need to get a good look at you
… my word … it's like he's here with me. like he's come back
after all these years. you remind me of an old old friend. a friend
who's been dead and gone for decades … why it really is quite
uncanny, i know you're not him but you look so … so … so …
much … if i didn't know better i'd say you, young man, were
wearing his face. if i didn't know better i'd say you, young man,
had stolen his face.'

why does this keep happening to me?
third time this week.
twelfth time this month.
thirty third time this year.
probably hundredth time overall.

people see what they wanna see, i guess
and what they wanna see is a dead guy who they haven't seen in
years.

and for some reason a lot of people see their dead friends in me.

either that or maybe i look exactly like just one dead guy. who
was pretty well travelled and travelled to exactly the same places
as me. maybe i'm coincidentally retracing all his steps, or maybe
he's guiding me from the other side, using me to haunt his
friends. today i haunted the costa coffee queue. tomorrow, who
knows.

HOW I GOT TO THE TOP

i climbed outta that primeval sludge with one impulse and one
impulse only: to fuck you in the mouth. my ancestors were slugs,
i was raised by amoeba, and forced to work on a chain gang,
snorkel nosed at the bottom of a festering swamp, while bright
fishes with exotic scales made bowtie patterns in the clean water
a mile above my head, i chiselled my way free and charmed
my way to the top, sleeping with who i had to and keeping
one japseye open the whole time cause you never know when
trouble is coming, least of all when you're on your back, and
i'm not proud of what i had to do but i did it all the same and
if given the choice and i'd do it all a-gain and i grew gills outta
sheer force of will and i sprouted legs to walk outta the water, up
onto that beach with my scaly head held high and i stuffed my
fist into the chest of a nearby sunbather, ripped out his lungs and
connected 'em to airways cut fresh into my goddamn fish cheeks
cause this fucking planet ain't gonna get the better of me, and i
walked into that beach hut with my lizard dick swinging and i
said 'how many clams for those bermuda shorts, you sunburned
floatation device with a pulse?' and i walked outta there the envy
of every ape in the joint cause i was less evolved but chewing my
way past them up the food chain, and i went straight to the top
of the bell tower, to demand the helm position at this goddamn
company, and i strode down the board table like a pussywalk
wiggling everything i got, and that fat fart bag squirmed n
squalled like a schoolgirl as i dug my lizard tongue direct into his
gargling throat, head held tight in a pincer vice grip cause i'm
centuries worth of strong and i made a meal deal out of his vocal
chords and the greying cancer cells that incased them. spitting
phlegm onto the office floor, watching his eyes rock n roll back
into his skull and life leave his body limp. well it was all i could
do to stop myself from punching the air … CEO, and i ain't
even bin on this planet five minutes.

i'm cuckoo. like a clock.
i've clocked off. i'm out of my cage.
i'm drink driving. i'm driving
this keyboard drunk. again.
i am pretending the words
are a road. again. i have road rage.

i was driving, now i'm parked.
i have been pulled over by a state trooper.
hello. r u driving the keyboard drunk again?
yesss. i am driving the keyboard drunk again.

WHY I LOOK LIKE A FOETUS

i look like a foetus
because i am still in denial
about having been born.

i was at a bar, three beers in, late afternoon, place almost abandoned. not only at the bar, but sitting up at it. it was june or maybe a warm day in may. i don't remember. electric power was surging on and off. the neon lights of the beer logos would be on, the jukebox blaring away for the length of one song, then the bar would be plunged into silence and dark. 'goddamnit' the barkeep would say, disappearing backstage to flip some breakers, we'd have song and light for another 2 mins, then the whole thing would power down again.

on / off . on / off . on / off.

for an hour.

'just leave it off' i said. the barkeep disappeared backstage for the 30th time. he came back. tried to resume his stock check by electric lights. it happened again. and now he was in a huff. you could kinda see what his parents musta been like when they got mad.

'i'm just gonna leave it off' he said, as though it was his idea. he propped open an emergency exit to let some light in. and i listened to my tinnitus pretending it was music.

an old guy shuffled in and took the barstool next to mine. 50 empty seats. howbout that?

we sit shoulder to shoulder in silence. then he says 'i'm doing okay!'

we sit in silence a little more. 'your outfit really suits you, it really does.'

i look down at my black jeans. same ones i'm wearing right now, probably. otherwise it was pink converse and a black t-shirt with the logo of the place i worked at the time – a bowling alley. you wouldn't really call it an outfit. i smiled to accept the compliment.

'oh you rascal, you' the old boy said, staring straight ahead, not even looking at my outfit.

he ordered two scotch and waters from the barkeep. when they came i thanked him but he didn't you're welcome me. he also didn't slide one in front of me. perhaps they're both for him, i thought. why not order a double? it's cheaper and comes in the same glass!

he asked me what i had been doing in sidcup. and i hadn't been
to sidcup in four years, and only then for a day, so i piped up to
tell him so. he turned to me, indignant, and said 'do you mind?'
when his eyes made contact with mine i saw utter conviction
in his greying pupils. weathered skin like bruises round the
eyesockets. he gestured to indicate a person sitting directly ahead
of him (standing on the other side of the bar maybe?), who i
could not see.

'well …' i said, taking it in. 'if you … two … wanted a private
conversation you didn't have to sit so close to me'
'well where else would you suggest we sit?' and then he gestured
to the almost completely empty bar.

i nodded an apology and he turned back to face forwards, slid
the second drink across the bar into empty space, and resumed
the conversation he was having with no one.
i watched him listen intently to shocking anecdotes, rapt by
sage points and ingenious observations and witty repartee … all
coming outta the mouth of someone i couldn't see.
i watched the man conversing with dead space, and thought, this
isn't so very different from what i'm doing right now as i write
this.
i pushed my bar stool back and stood up. the man rolled his eyes
sarcastically towards dead space. presumably his companion
smiled and rolled their eyes as well. it didn't feel awesome to be
teenager'd by these two ancients. one of whom was invisible.
and then, as if they hadn't just sassed me, he asked all innocent
'where ya going? don't let us old codgers frighten you away.'
'gotta stretch the legs.' i said.
  by now the place had started to fill in a little bit. i walked to
the other end of the bar and ordered another beer and watched
some people try and play the fruit machines that weren't getting
any electric power. out the fire escape was a patch of concrete,
sun had moved on so it was now a warm spot of afternoon
shade. perfect for a sensitive little pink-skinned pinko like me. i
grabbed an empty chair from a long table nearest the door and
dragged it towards outside. halfway out the door, the lady sitting
alone at the other end of the table screeched and bellowed 'can't
you see someone is sitting there?'

'ahh-shit sorry!' i said, dragging the chair back inside. the old woman was short and squat with a big black hat. she rushed over with handkerchief in hand and started tending the bruises of her friend who i'd just dumped on the floor. 'shameful behaviour. shameful. izzy has been my friend for 45 years. izzy. izzy.'
'look i didn't see her there, i'm sorry'
she mumbled something into the deadspace about the invisibility of older women.
'sor-ry' i said again, trying to sound 0% sarcastic.
'oh. oh. oh. it's an american is it?' she hoarsed, hearing my accent. 'that explains the rudeness. that explains the rudeness. that explains it ... barkeep! barkeep!'
he came over, grinning wide and sided with the old ladies.
'these ladies are right. you are rude. probably because you're an american. these ladies have been customers for 45 years. i'm sorry ladies.'
i told him he was a dip-shit and moved towards the fire escape.
'you can't go out there. that's for staff cigarette breaks only. we're not insured or licensed for outside ...'
i told him he was a double dip-shit and took a seat at the very other end of the place. completely in darkness, a corner seat by the ladies room door, a table that nobody would ever choose unless they'd been hounded and shamed into sitting there. i made my way over there with hunched spine and flat feet, head bowed down, trying to convey 0% sarcasm through my body language. and i was very careful to not bump into any invisible people. i slumped down at the crappy table.
after a few minutes i got up to take a leak, got to the urinal and realised it was a number two. so i went into the can and sat down and for all i know i sat ontop of someone who was already there and shat through them.
i came back and took a pull or two on my beer. listened to the fragments of conversations and laughter across the bar. these people were having better chats with their friends who either don't exist or don't exist anymore, than i have with people who are still here.
so ... i took a deep breath and i tried it.
i started asking questions to the empty chair across from me.
at first i felt stupid, and got no answer.

but after a time i had someone dialled in.
someone who i miss quite a bit, ya know.
we chatted for hours and i sank a few more beers.
i didn't start buying two at a time, cause my date didn't drink
booze when they was alive. and it's embarrassing enough to
order lime and soda for people who are still here.

ex-girlfriend used to refer to her snatch as an axe wound. was never pussy or vagina or garden or cave or crack or pocket or purse or salty-slit or second mouth or cooch or cooter or snatch. to her it was axewound axewound axewound. everytime: axewound axewound axewound. so i forged this kinda unhealthy association. ya know? made me think of *axe wounds* … as erotic.

so now i'm on the hunt for someone who has an actual axe wound. i can't get this idea out of my head. ya know, i'm hanging around at lumber yards, and following people down aisles in the hardware store … looking for first time axe buyers. following 'em home. parked outside, hoping they'e going to use the axe THAT night. praying they got some wood needs chopping right-a-way, ya know, before it gets water logged by rain. waiting for 'em to come outta the house, watching 'em from my car, watching as they unwrap the new axe and set up some logs for the virgin swing, and ya know, i sit back and let 'em get a couple of good swings in, let 'em get their confidence up, i wait til they look like they're *really* winding back. like, they've split a couple of warmup logs, but THIS is gonna be the one, i wait for that babe ruth windup, for the axe head to be glinting in the last strains of dusk, for the backswing to begin and then: BLANG BLANG BLANG. i punch my car horn as hard as possible and watch as the person's head turns towards the noise, startled by my car horn, but the axe is already on its way down and the head of the thing near-misses the wood, bounces off the log, as one hand lets go the handle and the axe itself swings rogue through the air and plants its vicious blade with a slurping noise straight into the fatty tissue of the person's thigh or upper arm maybe, and i'm untangling myself from the seatbelt and running across the front yard, jumping over the sprinkler, kicking those pink flamingos to the ground for good measure, i come skidding to a muddy stop right next to this horrific accident. FUCK FUCK – HELP ME! the person screams with the wodden axe handle hanging out of them like they're a human lolipop, blood squelching round the sides of the entry wound, tear ducts doing their thing, pumping dime sized water droplets out onto the lawn, and i'm thinking 'with waterworks like that, man, your sprinkler is suddenly surplus to requirement ... what a waste of water' and i pull the axe outta the wound, i hold my new friend close, i unfurl my penis and insert it dozens of times into the wound.

and in the awkward beautiful moments to follow, the two of us curled together like stray pubes on god's bathmat ...

'what the hell did you do that for?' my new friend shudders ...

'o no ... did you say *fuck fuck – help me?*. i'm dyslexic. i thought you said *help help ... fuck me.*'

and then we cry.

each of us

for different reasons.

and as i walk away i'm thinking 'god, that's not even how dyslexia works'

you can get away with anything in this world.

so long as the person on the other end of it

is gullible.

speaking of gullible ... that's story is, uh,,, only partly true.

SPEND MONEY. SAVE MONEY. GAMBLE.

spend money. save money. gamble. take out a loan. buy a used car. don't smoke. keep hold of your belongings. keep your clothes on. you call *that* skin? why aren't you radiant? cover new ground. push ahead. spread risk. maximize returns. diversify. simplify. purify. hate your job. get a job. say goodbye. trust us. give yourself an energy boost. eat healthy. culture yourself. feel observed. be ok with surveillance. feel overwhelmed. let us help. volunteer … volunteering improves your employability. consider the beauty of death. forget the certainty of death. rock out! shock yourself. creep yourself out. be vigilant. be on the lookout for danger. imagine kidnapped children. imagine *this many* kidnapped children. fear for your children. fix your broken child. fix your broken inner child. pay for private healthcare: your child is worth it. pay for private: you are worth it. pay for private: jump the queue. pay for private: your time is worth it. feel content. celebrate female solidarity. swim with whales. come to sri lanka. don't smoke. you are better than average. you are better than average so prove it. remember this in case of emergency. respect property. respect that this cost us money. purchase security. educate yourself. understand that things sometimes go wrong. do not sue us if things go wrong. do not be a hero. put your faith in the system. stand still. move if necessary. define necessary. help us to help you. speak clearly. state the emergency but don't panic. acknowledge the emergency but don't let the emergency effect you. get out of the way. don't stand here. don't smoke. follow instructions. interact with the machine. do not die on our property. do not steal. fear the bureaucracy that enforces this. get in touch. feel as though you can influence us. trust us. be impressed by the complexity of the machine. appreciate how difficult our jobs are. don't punch the staff. don't smoke. if you do smoke: feel bad about it. don't break and enter. don't break. don't die on our property. fear the danger. get away to the country once in a while, it's what your soul wants. get away to a small town once in a while, it's what happy couples do. sometimes things are inconsistent. don't blame us when you are late. connect. be afraid: 400 volts. trust us … that's a lot of volts. don't inconvenience the people who live here. geography is all around you. know where you are.

feel welcome. donate. don't make a mess here. treat yourself on saturday. treat yourself every saturday. why go to a bar when you can go to brussels for the price of *a round of drinks?* go to brussels. buy a round. get a job. don't slip. buy a sofa. once you have bought a sofa you will be able to relax. save money. have respect for motherhood. put on your brakes. lift this flap only if necessary. your health is fragile. be afraid. pay us. pay us. let us vaccinate you. get a job. buy a sofa. pay us. get a job. use this hammer when the time is right. be a hero. break the glass. don't sit here. don't die. you can't sit here. you can't afford to sit here. stay seated … somebody is already shitting where you want to shit. be thankful you don't have a brain tumour. yet.

SLIME GLAND FROM SEPTIC THROAT

jump skipped town like a hot rod, fist pumped, blood beat
temple like an ingrown ipod, sight be told she squirts into the
wind, a yellow trickled she-wad and floats to heaven's gate on
castration fantasy, purple tarpaulin st penis breath icloud and
damn that shit is so loud. she's facing off against skyscrapers.
morning papers ain't taught her nothing but who to fear and
what to hate and what she wore and what he ate. 2 fingers ain't
enough to change your mind. 2 fingers ain't enough to blow
you away. how many little fingers does it take to blow your
mind? teaching historical fiction n soft fact, taut like the skin of
a drum, a penny wouldn't bounce, shit sheets done stained in
my cum and tonight i pray for you, i play the gimp, i pray for
you and we rip off & kill your pimp. i ain't braggin but it were
easy, that fatso godangled as he fell like a wimp, coke stained
nostrils woulda pissed himself if his dick coulda got limp. i ain't
paranoid, it's simple, the mothership is coming. my hair-do ain't
hair: it's an antennae helmet for beaming back signals to the
home planet. and when that matriarch goes off in the sky you
don't wanna be beneath her. trigger empty barrel gloopy pupils
like ink in water getting kinda bugged out cause i know you're
somebody's daughter. a love wound across yr chest like pearls.
staring death in the dick til his pubic hair curls. from a pulpit
duck-down scrawling vomit on the preacher. she sachets across
the room with an empty heart. a loud buzz like swarm and he
fuck buckles into the room and she says 'sorry i was showerin'
when you rang' and that's a lie and she says 'baby, if god didn't
want me to lie he wouldn't have given me shame and a mouth.'
the truth got rotted out like a fungal sprout of varicose veins all
over her youth. suck-suck see-see lamps roil in their sockets and
the trucker pushes the accelerator down all the way, he drives a
14 wheeler big rig blinfolded, dick stiff like a corpse, cock harder
than algebra, he's doing 500 miles per hour in a big rig, straight
thru stopsigns, crunching over bodies at the crosswalk by the old
age home, swerving to hit children outside the pre-school, sharp
lefthand turn in his mile-long rig, time to disappear, go where
the cops won't follow, into a so called bad neighbourhood,
lookin' for a so called good time, cos major tom has got a minor
problem, it's smack history month, the inner city is all loaded up

on junk, kingdom come, kingdom came on my face, kingdom
never calls me back, chosen one chosen race, n there's nothing
below zero, nothing lesser than none. this prison planet, this
cop colony, kick out the bars, it's closing time on your ideas.
they brought you to your knees. and they brought your knees
home to mama in a leadlined box. voicebox shortcircuits: *put yr
hands behind yr head. put yr hands behind yr head.* he reached for his
weapon and they shot him, they shot him, he was reaching – we
all saw that, we did. milky ropes cream-blood spilled like a '55
hollywood production. luck is in he breathes and spit sticks to his
lips like glue from a gun. and a powder keg of you know what?
is ticking on the table between us … and it's a waiting game of
who blows which match and which brought the better batch
ba-ba-ba-boom out blows the window, night sky too many colours
like a tie dye tee shirt, you are sucked outta that window, you fly
feet first towards the sun, across the dkny-sky, ice dripping your
wings as you hurtle across space the fingernails are sucked right
off your fingers, your body liquifies in your space suit, you bloat
and explode, caked coated vocal jazz chords like bondage ropes
taut round a little girl begging to be taught a lesson bruised and
blistered cos we pretend to be sisters and ecstasy nay nirvana
nay paradise awaits you above the ceiling tiles of the clouds.
you have arrived. this cliche falls like rain, back to planet earth,
and the future is a flicker on my tongue. i swallow liquor out of
the bottle mouth and throttle my pipes. come inside n don't ask
no permission, slip inside to where the buck stops. hand over
will. free or otherwise. til the lake is empty and entropy sings
envy to an empty auditorium, this amphibian crawls slime gland
from a septic throat, he tears up his own face and inside him is
a little girl. out spurts little girl liquids. she squints and wipes the
slime casing from her freckled face, shakes the lizard skin off,
it evaporates, her cooter glands glow pink, *is this* she says and
smirks in a loop so clipped so degrading we push it all the way
to clipping all the way into the red to induce tripping, falling out
of planes and being sucked (backwards) up into the sky, what
good is a parachute if you are a falling dead weight, like a bag
of bombs from an airlock, this man is killing himself in reverse,
sucked up into the sun, pierced a small implosion little incision
tiny incisor tiny inside her, come inside and melt with me,
don't ask for permission, come inside, come inside, thought got

think-stretched to breaking, gun barrel wheels into the mouth, a muzzle inside, firing pin number – just 9 – 1 – 1 – hammer blows your tongue off and a hole in your cheek. you turn swivel spitting blood tooth splinters cut throat weak hands jam safety switch push as hard as possible and push your face right down through the barrel impaled in the veiny face hole in front smoke rising like a blunt in this heartless wordless deathsong now. you rise from the ashes like a bluebird soul. naked dick sips urine like fine wine just bad luck enough. luck lies in a pool of what has been spilled and guess what? death is just a corpse with a leaky dick like a trigger juicing x chromosomes into piss stained y fronts. and he cries 'here goes everything and here comes nothing' as a lightning bolt shoots out from under his fingernail and dances across the room, hits you square in your weak spot: disease flirts death dimension. demented smoke inhale snort the short nub of what's left of your brain. your skull is turned inside out and pulled out yr nose by a fondue fork, deflating like a popped balloon, your head turns inside out wilts like fruit and falls off. whoops! you're dead again. years later as a headless cadaver riding underage pussyfarts like wild horses in the afterlife, you cum and dismount, then pork a pig in the colon and do a line off the swine, and look up to see the little girl from inside the lizard. you two make it. she is of age now. so it ain't no – don't stop – don't stop – don't stop – don't stop – don't stop – don't stop. giggle baby blue messiah. your grandmother is masturbating in her grave. all stoned like a commemorative plaque. she cures gingivitis. 'here comes nothing, here goes everything.' a blast from underneath death's fingernail impales the sky on a lightning fork. good looking trucker called buck pulls into truck stop sweaty, big rig 14 wheeler, liquor on lips, waffle pocket stained from a second breakfast cause killing makes me a hungry man and i got 2 corpses in the back and a pretty one ridin' up in the cab. drove all night to get to nowhere. 6 days outta rehab. rehabitual – not my scene, teen, not my bitch-uation – and lick a trigger erupt. and kick back up front like a shotgun. you ride like a passenger in your own fucking life. kickback relax. kickback shotgun leaves a bruise the bullet path bullet pathways to the brain. the killer clears his throat. drumming hatred on esophagus. just begging for a softer kiss. the big rig engine roar and lights go out. parkinglot in darkness.

now the killer is dumping the bodies. and corpse 2 jumps up
outta that ditch re-animated. and the bruise disappears from the
face like falling dirt. the bullet speeds tip ass-backwards into the
exit wound, through the skull out the che guevara martyr dot in
hindu spot bullseye centre of the brainhead, blood gets sucked
up into the wound as the bullet flies across the parking lot and
right back into the gun.

the killer was me all along.
the villain was me all along.
the killing by this here goddamn villain …
was done by me all along.

corpse 2 is now back alive.
stumbling bambi-legged in the parking lot.

the face wound closes up like it was never there.
re-born.
crime undone …
it's time for me …
time for me …
time for me …
time … to fucking run.

THIS ORGANISM HAS OUTLIVED
THE PLAN

can't hide from no truth no lie too wide to hear tonight, right
here we hide in hope and cling to dead ringers and songs sung
by dead singers, i fear no feral love no aerial too long to get this
transmission, what say you god, what answer you pose like a
question cause it turns out wrong is right, black is just another
shade of grey, promise to never die, to never say 'enough' cause
this buffet is the best in town, this buffet got 'em coming for
miles, cause this species is hungry and we never close – will you
give it up? will you give it all away? – this sentence my enemy
as it turns on me and licks out my wounds like a lover that you
trust, but do you love me for the right reasons? do you love
me for the right reasons? i ain't no hairspray side saddle rodeo
clown but i am a girl for all seasons. wriggle free from other
truths this mind is sick, this mind is infected, i got two uninvited
guests drilling quests right inside cause this this mind is infected
by business and science, i never asked to be born, i never asked
to be born, i never asked to be, this man is jumping up buildings,
killing himself in reverse, i will leave no stain on this world,
i promise, let these words be my last train leaving this world,
cause you and i will not make our father's father's mistakes.
heavy whisper breathe into sister-girl 'man made evil man and
it's bubbling up inside of me.' ... the ceiling is blown off and god
storm reaps the lightning air, can you taste the storm? i feel ill,
i feel ill, eyeballs turn yellow and mucus blows from my throat,
can you fix-save me? else save me a bullet? or is there only a
french maid in the chamber? and i never got bravery running
in my veins, my vanity is unfair, my mind races somehow outta
gas, i got a brain that plays host to ad copy and guilt and gag
reels 25 hrs a day, like there's a ted talk in my mind and the guy
is wrong about everything. another hero dies face down in the
mud, loveletter pinned to his bible pinned to his community
lovin chest. that symbolism is lost on no one, that symbolisms
is lost, full stop, full stop. a hero never arrives at the lips of hell,
no boat, even our slave ships are sinking. protest banner flies
cause truth is no spoke in that word, she said 'no matter what,
you strut your fucking stuff, you say that word n we shut you
down, we retaliate hate with hate or else we pay you to shut up'.

but currency gotta bad name, no worry at all, we'll just rebrand
money cause spin doctor says no sickness is too ill. no germ he
can't kill with a pill and a whitewash laxative swill. you do not
own your own body you do not own your own mind you do not
own your own body you do not own your own mind you do not
own your own self. you have been ad-copied into existence by
pre-programmed prophesy and pupil blowing image in hi def.
sorry to break it to you. you are broken. and back in the real
world there ain't never enough, cause there's always a tomorrow
and we need fuel to get there, set the controls for the heart, my
son. the heir to my shitstain'd throne, toilet sick got splatter
pattern like a dog ate a firework and puppy is now jackson
pollock poop-splatter on a porcelain canvas. a peeping tom
neighbour takes notes on my form. tells me i'm calloused from
the heels up, blistered from the fire, ligament flames lick thunder
hips from black boy lips i bought online to upgrade this body.
this pathetic carcass that i'm trapped in. this sunburnt flotation
device with a pulse. i ain't even human no more or at least that's
the plan. break me open and stuff me full of perfect. no love
til perfect self achieved. no love til perfect match made. and i
picture no face but yours, baby, sorry, reader, sorry, audience.
i cast a lover in the mould you set. i cast a new lover in the
shape you leave behind. cause connection has timed out. and
the harder they come the harder they fall in love. love is locked
forever behind a door made of flattering reflections of yourself.
crawl creeping til noose goes slack around a slacker. tired brit
slang 'knackered': exhausted, tail pipe taped to her lips, i am
sucking exhaust fumes like perfume on a lovers neck. we shed
what's over, we shake loose the artefacts we no longer need, this
organism has outlived the plan, no safety net, all god's have been
suspended, ours had a p45 dismissal slip and fell out of heaven.
and they put video cams in your eye holes, recording everything
that you do and do not like. and you can dial m for misogyny
or d for direct action to watch that office sleaze have his spinal
column ripped out when the jackboots kick the window in, but
first they cut off his penis and they call him faggot as he tries to
sew it back on. and the technology that serves all this up doesn't
care which side you're on. funny cause it rings true, funny cause
it is true. a cane becomes a noose around your neck, bugs bunny
battered, eyes bugged, daffy lisps 'stupid bunny … tricks are for

kids' except he can't say that cause his spinal cord broke, neck
rung like a real duck, like a sitting fuck, daffy makes crispy hoi
sin pancake fodder or duck l'orange. that's french fry for fuck
you, they pour wine in the streets like motor oil as mohammed
flips through penthouse forum looking for a hookup or to flick-
off to some retrograde erotica and just who do you pray to when
the sky is a wound? who do you pray to and who pays you?
mohammed ali, mohammed ala, mohamad falalala, that ain't
funny. don't make jokes about nothing outta your reach. your
asshole n your cock and your other short comings are all you
get to comment on. else you we blow you away, float up into
the night of the short stubby knives, all covered in blubber, the
night they reclaimed mother, salt stained her face with tears, let
us fuck no longer into existence the unasked for unborn while
we ravage the ones who are already here, battalions fed feet
first into the fire, another clone race smelted down, molten melt
and long forgot, forget me-knots in nooses doublespeak truces
disguise a white flag flown in fear, no choice but to admit 'things
don't look good, i ain't no betting man but if i was i'd bet my
bottom dollar on any horse except this one' cause nevermind
the handbasket … this is hell ala carte. no window dressing
or carrots cut into the shape of anything but carrots cause
they confiscated our knives on the way into this theatre, metal
detectors detecting weapons of every size and did you pack your
ball bag yourself sir? what about those bags beneath your eyes?
what about those bags you call your seven wives? i live a dual
life, that is i duel with myself like errol flynn, falling off carboard
pirate sets, internet girl logs-on to get-off on pirate sex, and
where do i get off / where do i get off / where do i get off / let
me tell you: i get off here. this is my stop.

full stop = •

WHOOPS! COLON CANCER

i briefly dated a guy who could fart smoke rings. when we broke up i wished colon cancer on him.

and this year he got it. or at least that's what his last email said.

do i a) buy him some marlborough branded underwear b) start mourning or c) hastily retract every cruel thing i've ever said before everyone i know starts dropping dead?

you buy yourself a new what-have-you. and you carry that what have you with you. so you always have your what have you with you. *hey, do you have a what-have-you with you?* yes! i always have my what-have-you with me. i don't leave home without it cause that would make it a what-i-don't-have-with-me, defeating the purpose of having a what-have-you at all. no darn point in having a what-have-you if you don't have it with you. have you got a what-have-you? *yes … but i don't have it with me.* how can you have a what have you and not have it with you? *that's why i asked if you have a what have you, cause i have a what have you but i don't have that what have you with me.* well, how do i know you have a what have you if you don't have it with you? how long have you had a what have you? *i've had a what have you long enough to not need to have a what have you with me all the time.* well … what have you got with you? *i have … with me … half a what have you.* half a what have you? *half a what you.* well where's the other half? *i haven't seen it.* you haven't seen the other half of your what have you? *(shake head)* hey reader! have you seen the other half of this guy's what have you? well, have you? *hey hey hey, shhhh. why don't we just share your what have you? you have a whole what have you with you.* but if we share my what have you which i have with me, we will only have half a what have you each. *no you'll only have half a what you, i'll have half of your what have you and the half a what have you i have with me.*

look … between us we have one and a half what have yous. but we are two people. *no we're not. you're just a person i made by turning my head.* i am? … *yeah.* so we are one person creating the illusion of two people. which averages out at one and a half people? *correct-a-mundo!* so we actually have the right amount of what have yous for the number of people we are. … *only if you share with me your what have you. because right now you have a what you with you and i have only half a what have you with me.* okay, well, let's share mine then … (they do) wait … now you have two half a what have yous. and i have only one half a what have you. *yeah, but in total we have the right amount now.* we had the right total before, now you have more than half the what have yous. *no … i don't have more than half a what have you. i have two different half a what have yous, that's all i have.* but that makes … look … cause … we both need to share both of our what have yous we have with us, so we can both have one half of our one and a half what have yous we have with us. (pause) so … come on … (pause) fine then … i'll just take back my whole what have you and you can be the one with half a what have you again. *nope. you can't, cause i have half your what you have you and you can't have it back.* wha … ? but that isn't fair! *well … ya know, this never woulda happened if you hadn't a had a what have you with you …*

MY MASKS

there's this little room just over there. i wait in there for you to
arrive.
i keep each one of my facial expressions.
hung up on a hanger.
and i uh. iron them
before each performance.
gotta look my best.

TEQUILA WORM

2008,
interstate 90, new york state thruway
buffalo, one mile from niagara falls

cop car swerved to the shoulder of a 3 lane highway. the i-90.
gravel sprayed the treeline. detective kim rex had laughed coffee
out of her nostrils and damn near crashed the car.

also in the car was an actor doing a ride along, studying her for a
part in a moving picture.

the actor was laughing a very fake laugh in accompaniment to
kim's aria of genuine guffaw.

what a fuckin' phoney kim rex thought to herself as she wiped
snowball sized tears from her face.

'so umm can you tell me about … could you illuminate for me
… like … my character like is … like meant to be a merciless
killer. so. could you like give me an instance of a time like, in
terms of you being a like killer?'

kim scanned her memory … every cop remembers their first
kill.

her eyes misted over, pupils shrank to pinholes. the ride along
fired up his dictaphone.

eventually kim spoke:

'it was back in the '90s when i was a wide eye'd cadet, younger
than you are now. it was at a motel called arkona. niagara falls,
on the canadian side. a cheap r-rated place, thin walls, colour tv,
jacuzzis in the bathrooms. a stone's throw from the stripclubs.
i um, i had a lead on a child pornographer, real scum of the
earth, real human debris. name of catalomaxahyde rondagooey

faliochesip allagarundi. … not a name i'll forget anytime soon. easy to remember because it rhymed with the location. the arkona motel was on a lane called *lundy*. and that rhymes … catalomaxahyde rondagooey faliochesip allagarundi … lundy. see? easy!

so, i get the tip-off that this child pornographer has crossed the border to do a hookup with his canadian distributor, now that officially makes it a canuck problem not a yanky problem, but corruption in the canadian force runs so deep we knew that sharing intel with them would be tipping our hand to the enemy. i was fresh faced and young and plenty anonymous. so i went undercover across the border dressed as a cocktail waitress. i wore a wire but the cops monitoring the wire were in a van on the other side of the border, legally they couldn't cross into OPP territory, and the signal was a crackly mess at that distance, kept crapping out and crapping in and crapping out again, so i was essentially operating alone *and* without a safety net. so i make my way to case the joint, i let myself in through an open window, flea bit motelroom, like i said, sleazebag payola snoozing at the desk in a bad toupee, on the bed was a huge briefcase full of vhs tapes containing a phantasmagoria of the worst crimes imaginable. i unspooled some of the film from one of the tapes and held it up to the light to verify i had the right room, the right guy. and i viewed one single frame of this shit … and i swear i will never be the same, i will never unsee it. i will never unlearn the exact depth of hell. i aged ten years in an instant. any hope i had for humanity atrophied. i put the vhs tape down on the bed. approached the sleeping sleaze at the rolltop desk. grabbed him by his cheap tie. throttled him and shoved his face down on to his paperwork. his blubbery cheeks squished against the open pages of his day planner. i shoved his face down hard into thursday and friday. i drove my knee into his back, and parked it right at the base of his spine, twisted his arm til i heard the creak of old bones. his other hand groped around wildly, trying to punch and clutch at me. it landed on my groin, *feel me up*, i thought. *i dare you. better me than a child, you won't ruin me by brushing your panicked hands against my grandest of canyons.* so i pressed his head harder into the desk. he turned to look up at me and beg for mercy. tomorrow's appointments had transferred themselves onto his forehead. backwards. my pubic hair bristled as he flailed past it. i could hear the tick of his wristwatch now. so i pressed my mound into his wrist in order to silence the watch. we held eye contact and a bruise formed on his face. a bead of sweat rolled down his forehead, through the ink stain, taking some of the P from 230 PM with it. i ripped one arm up to his shoulder blades and heard the bone snap, watched the bone pierce through the broken skin, through the shirt, through the sleeve of his $4 tuxedo. he let out a throaty bray, his other hand fumbled furtively in a drawer. i kicked it, hard as i could. i probably should've waited til the hand produced a gun or a knife or a grenade from the drawer – that would have been fair play – but i wasn't feeling fair and this was work for me … not play.

his furtive hand contorted from the toe'd blow. so i kicked it again, this time crunching it against the edge of the desk, stamping on it with the 7 inch heel of my leather mules, my undercover-as-a-cocktail-waitress-shoes … really tried to break the fingers. he let out a wheeze and one of the fingers fell off.

i let go of his cheap tie, it slacked from his strangled throat & his fat face fell THUD to the desktop.

i rolled the rolling top of the roll top desk down onto his head. gdddd-gdddd-gdddd // BANG!

rolled that thing down and closed it.

once. twice. gdddd-gdddd-gdddd // BIFF!

three times. gdddd-gdddd-gdddd // BASH!

i rolled up the rolltop of the rolltop desk to investigate the damage … his head was split open now, big cleave running east to west, right across the middle like the equator. or like the canadian / american border for that matter. blood poured out of the cleave, he turned his head to look at me while he expired.

and the blood washed the rest of tomorrow's appointments away.

'clear your schedule' i hissed. 'cause from now on your life is gonna be death. 24hrs a day'

i rolled the roller of the rolltop desk back up.

into the unrolled position.

i embraced the body. let it go limp in my arms.

i let go the body. it crumpled to the floor.

i took a seat on the musty bed. it stank of bleach and cigarettes and the last guy's semen.

i thought about taking the case of videocassettes back across the border with me. about turning them in at the precinct. that's what i was supposed to do. that's what was agreed. i thought about the twisted fucks who worked above me: the detectives and lieutenants and worst of all, the commissioner. crooked and perverted, almost all. i imagined the tapes going missing from the evidence room, as narcotics often did. i imagined those tapes being copied on double decker vhs machines, copies leaked onto the blackmarket, the originals deposited back in the evidence room. i thought about the money the opportunists above me would make by circulating these tapes. and about the black ooze spreading tv to tv, eyeball to eyeball, soul to soul. i pictured the black ooze tarnishing all that it touches.

i found a cigarette lighter in the corpse's pocket, dumped the suitcase and all its contents into the jacuzzi tub in the bathroom. it was a heartshaped liptstick red tub. rust around the taps and chlamydia cultures festering in the plughole. the videotapes wouldn't light at first – plastic burns, but only once a fire is blazing. i went back out to the desk looking for kindling, was about to crumple up the corpses dayplanner and paperwork,

my fingers were an inch from doing so when i realised ... this
paperwork is evidence that could help us catch more of these
guys, this dayplanner may have the whereabouts of other
hookups in other towns, it may even have phonenumbers
and addresses for child pornographers in all 50 states, and all
however-many canadian provinces ... this could be the ticket to
bringing a whole basket of these snakes out of the longgrasses
and into the courtrooms. and if not the courtrooms, then at least
a few more might find their way into caskets.

i looked around the room for a newspaper or magazine for
kindling and found none ... i was about to peel off some
wallpaper when i remembered ... the bedside table drawer.
opened it up and bingo: the gideon's bible. even an r-rated
motel like the arkona is blessed by the father the son and the
holy spit.

the good book went up in flames page by page, verse by
verse, prophet by prophet. and it took the child porno tapes
with it.

as the fire blazed in the bathroom i went back into the bedroom,
checked the corpse's pulse.
gone.

i uncrumpled him from the floor, blood was saturating the
carpet. i positioned him back in the chair, leaning over the
desk, in the position i'd found him. his head was lolled over. i
balanced a pen in his now crippled, mangled, 4 fingered hand.
the toupee fell off and hit the floor. gangland tattoos like a
bullseye allover his scalp. and it was when i saw the bullseye on
the top of his head that i got the idea ...

i checked the drawer to make sure he hadn't been reaching for
a white flag. sure enough: a revolver. i checked the barrel: 3
bullets, 3 empty chambers. in an alternating pattern right around
the circle, girl-boy-girl-boy.

i studied his handwriting and did my best impression of it, scrawling a note on the last page of the dayplanner … *i can't do this anymore. i just found out i'm going to be a father. i don't trust myself. trust no one. see no evil. see no evil. see no evil. see no evil. see no evil. see no evil.*

i put the colour tv on. jeopardy was beamed into the room and i'll never forget what the question was: '60s icon, ex husband to cher, died in a skiing accident' said alex trebek. and whipfast this missouri housewife buzzes in and she says 'who is sonny bono?' and with that answer the housewife squeaked into first place and won the show. but the weird thing is … the really odd thing … is that sonny bono was still alive. this was the summer of '96. he didn't die til two januarys later.

the colour tv went to an advertisement for sunny delight. i turned the volume knob up to max. the tv rattled around in its stand, the speaker buzzing and distorting to the cheery sound of healthy people drinking soda marketed as orange juice.

i took a semen stained pillow from the bed, took the pillow case off it, and used it as a glove to grip the revolver. i placed the pillow over the corpse's head, opened the barrel and rotated it onto a loaded chamber. i closed the barrel and waited for the tv to go super loud. when a sitcom theme-song came crashing noisily into the room i fired a bullet down through the pillow, through the head of the corpse, through the desk and directly into my own foot. underneath my foot was carpeted floor then 24 inches of cement. that's where the bullet found its resting place. i staggered back and fell on the bed. i bit both my lips and stifled a scream, tried to bury that scream at the bottom of me. the scream came out my eyes in the form of tears the size of basketballs. they sloshed and bounced around the room. i directed my flow of tears to the cut in my foot and used the milk of my sadness to wash the wound.

i vibrated with pain and horror on the bed. amazed at my own power. the power i have to edit evil out of the world.

i went to the bathroom and watched the last embers of the plastic fire burn out, a dark green smoke billowing off the pyre. i stopped up the hole in my foot with toiletpaper, unspooling the toilet paper to make a makeshift bandage. doing so, i realised there was no reason to burn the bible … but then i picture dressing my wound with pages of leviticus and figured it was probably better this way round.

i limped out into the bedroom, turned the colour tv down to a more sensible volume. roseanne barr said something hilarious to john goodman, i'm sure. the studio audience guffawed. but i was too numb.

i opened up the window and lowered myself down to the courtyard below.

i took in the fresh air of the early evening. the sounds of colour tv leaking out of room after room after room. i moved down the coutryard, one foot hobbling, the other tiptoeing, both ankles bitching in 7" heels.

some hollywood greaseball was floating in the swimming pool, having downed a whole bottle of tequila. i drank in the scene. his greasy hair and canadian tan. the piss-green of the pool water. the early evening dying light.

he looked up when he saw me, told me what he'd done in a slur-blurry-no-diction voice.

'was it one of the tequilas with a plastic sombrero screwtop?' i asked.
'huh?' he said, rolling over in the water.
'was it one of the ones with a worm?' said a girl-voice from above.
a stripper was two floors up, watching us from her balcony. she had glittery makeup on and was lighting one cigarette off another.

the greaseball grunted and groaned and tried not to drown.
somewhere in there he answered our questions but my mind was
pounding so i didn't hear what he said.

'why would you go and drink a whole bottle anyhow?' i asked,
trying not to look suspicious with a bleeding hole in my foot.

the greaseball cocked his neck and looked showpony proud.
he said of how he'd be playing a heroin user in a major motion
picture later that year, and how the sensation of heroin use
is similar to that of drinking a whole tequila bottle and then
floating in a motel swimming pool.

'the bottle plus the room? that's more expensive than heroin.' i
said.

'and less like heroin than heroin.' the stripper said.

'yeah but it's legal.' he said.

'for now.' the stripper said. 'cops'll get to it eventually. cops'll get
to all the fun eventually.'

the greaseball floated like a piece of driftwood with a good
agent.

the stripper rolled her eyes at me and blew a dragon snort of
nicotine smoke out of her nostrils. i smiled and watched her
drink my outfit in. she smiled back at me in a way that made
it clear she bought my costume. *we are in the same club*, her face
seemed to say.

she asked my name and i made one up. said i was from
out of town. a long way from home. said i was from upper
saskatchewan. she said she was from just a few blocks away,
lived in this neighbourhood her whole life sofar. i thought about
asking why she was renting a motel room so close to home then
realised i already, pretty much, probably, knew the answer.

'they make a lot of movies in toronto now.' the stripper said.
'ontario is basically california without the weather …' she ashed
her cigarette over the balcony. '… so he could be telling the
truth.'

the greaseball couldn't hear us by now cause he was half
underwater, the waves lapping in his ears. 25 ounces of tequila
sloshing around inside him. and for all we knew a tequila worm
was swimming in his stomach.
he groaned into the early evening sky, as if to demonstrate how
messed up and junk sick he was. to play act his intoxication. to
show us how fruitful he was finding this character research.

the stripper rolled her eyes.

the greaseball pulled himself up outta the pool, his swimtrunks
rode down his legs as he emerged from the water, collecting like
shackles at his ankles. so, he stood up on the cement buck naked
from the ankles up. the hazy light glowed off his canadian tan.

god what a small and spindly penis i thought. *and no nipples at all …?*

i squinted and realised i'd got the image wrong. i was looking at
the back of him, hence the no nipples. and the small and spindly
penis was in fact … a tequila worm crawling out of his butthole.

the greaseball bent over to yoink his trunks up. fumbled with the
soggy fabric. and while doubled over, he vomited lightly onto
the tiled poolside.

and the worm arched itself up like a tiny question mark rising
from the man's exit pipe.

with charisma like that, i thought. *not long before the worm gets an
agent.*

i waved 'bu-bye' to the stipper's balcony but she was gone.

i hobbled round the side of the motel and hitchhiked back to the
border.'

rex's trenchcoat was now fully soaked with tears. like she'd gone through the car wash without a car.

the ride along clicked off his dictaphone and said 'wow'.

they sat in silence on the shoulder of the highway, cars, vans, trucks and buses all whipping by on the i 90.

after a few mins kim rex slurped some of her cold coffee, wiped her face dry.

the ride along spoke: 'uh yeah. uh. do you have. uh. thanks by the way. but uhh well, uh, do you have, like well like an example of like. more like. i mean my character is supposed to be a real throw the book meticulous, uhhh, i mean all brains and brawn and no heart. like uhh … i mean your story was rad n all. but it was really too emosh. see we're not going to be working with emotions. cause that's kinda false. so. like. but uhh like. i wanna know more about … how … um … cause my director is very much about …'

kim started the engine and the cruiser pulled out onto the i-90. she pointed it towards niagara falls. she was headed towards the canadian border for old times' sake.

AFTERLIFE

what if human consciousness carries on after electricity leaves the brain?
what if consciousness inhabits whatever we believed the afterlife would be?

so, a muslim may find themself in the long grasses, virgins splay'd in waiting, rubies growing up outta the ground, drinking from rivers of milk and feasting on infinite fresh fruit, and everything is so clean that pissing and pooping aren't even possible.
a jehova's witness would wake up 28-days-later style in their normal house in their normal bed, to find the world almost abandoned. cause this world is already a paradise and all that would be different is only jehova's witnesses would be around and all the animals would be set free and everybody would be blonde with blue eyes and stroking goats, and it would never rain.
and a jew may find themself inheriting a big chunk of paradise to personally own, on which all their dead relatives have sprung back to life. ... not a goy in sight. imagine a whole world where everyone had comic timing. even the clocks have comic timing in jew paradise.

and the atheists arrive into the nothing they promised themselves. and the agnostics sail the gushing oceans of the afterlife on a pirate ship shaped like a question mark, adrift in the chaos between belief systems, all the various heavens visible like islands on the horizon but never coming into focus. or maybe the agnostic inhabits the belief system she woulda-had had she believed. except it's the static-storm detuned television version. so she can't enjoy it cause everythings all fuzzy and out of focus.

and what if the judgements at the end are not made by an external force? what if the judgements are made by you? and religion just provides a schematic for figuring out whether you passed the test or not. if you are burdened with guilt, then you have mapped hell for yourself and you will inhabit it. if you believe in a clear white blissful nothing and you can honestly say you've earned that peace, welcome home.

there is no afterlife. if you leave here you are giving up on all there is.

dust to dust. dirt to dirt. dirt to dust. dust to dirt.

there is an afterlife. heaven waits for you if you hang in there.
and it is a crystalline sleek beauty carved exquisitely for you.
an ecstasy beyond description. and a peace balm for all the
wounds you got running through this world, barefoot wild and
naked, like you did.

your peace will come floating in on pillowy clouds. and ... gusts
of air-conditioning, and there's no junk mail, it's perfect. way up
there above the sky.

but it is only accessible if you wait for an invitation ... if you
try and jump the queue, and go there when you feel ready,
before you're chosen? if you decide when you leave earth?
then it's blast furnace after blast furnace after blast furnace after
blast furnace after blast furnace with no fire alarms, and no fire
escapes, just skin melting off you, regenerating and melting
off again, murderers in cages with bone bars, cauldrons of
piss served like soup, all the roses are dead and they smell of
burning hair, and black smoke fills your mouth, the ventilator
is connected to a car's exhaust pipe and everybody's got throat
cancer of the entire body ... and there's a super strong vaccum
that sucks your fingernails off your fingers, and daily butt rapings
come from a beast with horns, and a guido goatee, who's got
goat legs growing outta his kneecaps, and splayed hooves for
feet, and talons like samurai swords ripping open your back. and
if ya think you're getting off easy, cause ya reckon this rape is
coming from a goat penis sized penis, you're wrong cause in my
hell lucifer is a goat with a 45 inch penis, that's coked up, hard
for days, knobbled like treebark, dotted with genital warts, zebra
striped with herpe scars running spiral patterns round it like a
candycane at santa's grotto, it's as thick as a lamppost, maybe
there's a big tin sign the council bolted to it, displaying the speed
limit or a warning: humps for 1000 yards ...

and in case that sounds like fun to you?

it ain't no pornstars penis ... it's your dad's penis.

in my version of hell the goatman rapes you with your dad's
penis!

(cause it would be, wouldn't it? it's hell!)

THE DEVIL YOU KNOW

better the devil you know than the devil you don't … you don't know that! you don't know the devil you don't know. so, you don't know.

I LOVE YOU

i love you so much i'm not sure i wouldn't fuck our children. if there was a resemblance, if i saw enough of you in them, i'm afraid i'd have to get in them to get to that little bit of you. it's a good thing your twin brother died on his way to this planet, cause if you'd both survived i wouldn't trust myself around him either. i wouldn't *want* to fuck our kid. it's just … i know that i would.

BOMB SCARE

i'm at a table seat on a packed train. facing backwards as i type this. we are stopped between stations. somewhere like leeds or reading or bradford or newcastle or old castle. my geography isn't good. i just go where i'm told. i just go where i get booked. the other three people at my table are a family. they were happier before i sat down. mom (soz guv, british ... *mum*), dad and daughter. dad is long winded. i can tell from his briefcase. and b/c daughter is pretending to listen to him but has earphones in. visible to me, under her hair. mum is staring straight ahead at daughter, making 'playful' facial expressions designed to undermine daddy without him realising. expressions that say to daughter: the bond of your and my sex is stronger than the bond of his and my sex. the sex that made you is not as powerful as the sex that you are.

it's hard to tell if the daughter's coldness is b/c she thinks both her parents are lame or just the one. if it's just the one, my money is on him.

for what it's worth (and it's worth nothing. i know that.) i think both the parents are lame.

i picture myself sitting forward in my seat and leaning into their conversation, haulting both daddy's diatribe and mama's satirical eye-brow wigglin' commentary to say 'ahem ... excuse me ... you're *both* ... lame.'

but i can't risk it. i can't risk drawing attention to myself today. because today i've got a splodge of dried liquid latex on the groin of my jeans – i've washed them on 60, i've washed them on 90, i've washed them on 60 and then 30 to make 90, i've handwashed them ... well, i mean, i showered wearing them ... – this splodge. won't. budge.

i've got dried liquid latex on my groin and they'd never believe that's what it is. it looks even more like an ejaculation stain than an ejaculation stain does. it could never be passed off as toothpaste.

a screeching voice comes over the tannoy. something about have your tickets n passes ready. evidently this train is overstuffed and understaffed and this particular staff member (and *member* really is the right word for this one ...) can't see the funny side of anything. possibly b/c the funny side is obscured by all the sardine-packed-passengers.

she makes her way into our carriage – i'm in seat D48, in case you're autistic and care about that kinda detail – checking tickets with her hands, screaming with her mouth. berating people five rows away for not yet having their tickets in their hands, where she can see them. pretty soon we're the five rows away and then we're in the crosshairs. the closer she gets the more sorry for her i feel – she looks like her shift started in 2004.

'is this anybody's?' she screeches. 'ladies and gentlemen, this bag is unattended, ladies and gentlemen … is this anybody's?' being this close to her as she projects to address the entire carriage is like trying to nap with a fire alarm for a pillow. (fire alarm goin' off, natch)

none of us answers her. perhaps we are afraid to.

'is this … anybody's?' she screeches again, brayin' n kickin' in her virgin trains uniform. virgin trains. it's not hard to believe she's a virgin, cause even at this distance and fully clothed *all* my defense mechanisms are going up: cock shrivelling, turning inwards, sense of humour powering down, ability to hold eye contact annihilated. she's berating us like we are school children in the 1800's. i hide my knuckles in case she's packin' a cane.

i look up at the bag.

she screeches 'the bag, ladies and gentleman, it appears to be an orange bag.' (it is an orange bag) 'and it appears to have laptop cables coming out of it.' (it does have laptop cables coming out of it.) 'possibly contains a laptop.' (helluva detective).

she prods it with a finger as though it's about to explode.

'if nobody claims this bag ladies and gentlemen it will be treated as suspicious ladies and gentlemen … ladies and gentlemen that means the bag will be removed off of this train at the next station stop ladies and gentlemen. it will be destroyed by the security at the next station ladies and gentlemen. if it is yours speak up now. going once going twice …'

'it's mine!' … i heard myself say.

she sneered and leaned in, a blood vessel popped in her temple.

'why didn't you say so before?' she thundered.

'i'm hard of hearing' i said, which was all of a sudden kinda true.

she checked our tickets and moved out of our carriage. she sweated the small stuff all the way. i sat with the mysterious package in my lap, covering the latex stain on my not-so-mysterious package, all the way to my destination. the family of three sneered suspiciously – they were on the train before me so knew i was lying. but they didn't say anything ... too lame to stand up for what's right, i guess.

that night in my travelodge i dumped out the bag on the bed ... a tangle of wires, and sure enough, a laptop. a macbook XP5 ... jackpot.

next morning i sauntered into a pawnshop, played it real casual, but i secretly switched on my acting, and cooked up a helluva sob story: i said i'd fallen on hard times, i said the missus had the colick, i said there was one in the oven and another on the way, i said the foreman had laid me. and then laid me off. said men are pigs only interested in one thing ... not calling you. said the union was on strike, i was down on my luck. said i had a zero hour contract but even zero hours wasn't guaranteed. i said put yourself in my shoes, buddy. imagine not knowing at the beginning of the week whether or not you're gonna get the zero hours you're contracted to work, or none at all. ... and what's worse? i got loan repayments and romaine charges up the wazoo, my salad days are over, i said. i got an overdrawn paypal account, i'm an under-drawn character giving an overwrought monologue in an undercooked story that started out true but now isn't. i said, i remember what this town was like a generation ago, when us immigrants made this country what it is. where would britain be without the commonwealth? *(tap own chest)* and where would britain be without the commonpoor? *(point at pawnbroker)* ... without us canadians. and you ... uh?'
'albanians' said the pawnbroker, helpfully.
'... i mean, if us foreign people hadn't moved to britain and joined the armies, would britain have become the superpower

that it did 1000 years ago? would it have come to control so many of the world's resources? and all of its waves?'

'maybe not' said the pawnbroker.

'… and if us commonwealth hadn't woken up one day and realized we, ya know, *need* to be controlled. and if we hadn't *chosen* britain as our leader. ya know, invited them to be our dominatrix. and if we hadn't topped them from the bottom for so many years without them realising it, ya know, been real bossy bottoms, then without that *what* would britain even *be* right now?' and this next part was the real stroke of genius. i said 'and. if the albanians hadn't joined the EU when they did, and instead had chose to close themselves off all isolationist, with, ya know, military what nots, then maybe maybe maybe. it'd be britain banging on the door to get into albania right now.'

'yeah, fuck albania!' we both said in unison.

then we realised our mistake.

then the pawnbroker said this to me, she said:

'do you know what i think?'

'what?' i said 'what do you think?'

'i think that this country is a giant child, farting and puking at the same time, missing the toilet bowl and hitting europe.'

'yeah well that's one way of looking at it' i said.

i handed over the laptop bag.

'what's the password?' she said.

… stumped.

'uh … let me level with ya … *(whisper)* … i stole it.'

'hmm' she said. disapprovingly.

i explained the situation in full. she said one or two suspicious packages got pawned there most weeks. she said no harm in it cos the train company destroys the computer if they can't find the owner and what a waste of money that was. she said the train companies were over-zealous in these paranoid times.

but she also explained the computer was only worth 1/2 as much if she had to pay to get the password hacked. so i walked out

with a cool £100. not the coolest sum i could imagine ... but
pretty cool for basically no work.

halfway down the block i stared into the window of a gregg's
bakery, wondering what people eat in albania.
the concrete shook and car alarms started going off. i looked
back up the block to see a fireball where the pawnbroker used to
be.

i guess the train company wasn't *over*-zealous afterall.

i guess the train company was exactly the right amount of
zealous.

THE GREATEST MISTAKE I EVER MADE

i was using a drill one day to put up a set of shelves and drilled through the back of my own hand. when i pulled the drill bit out to investigate the damage i heard a distant rumbling sound and the rattling of ancient pipes. a great big jet of tar black oil came rushing out of the back of my hand. 'fuck' i said to the empty apartment. 'i've struck oil by drilling into the back of my own hand.'

i danced around the room in wild celebration, ecstatic as i pictured the mountains of money, the mercedes, the millionaire shortbread, me privately funding the cure for cancer and then being awarded all the future nobel prizes at once, i pictured the extravagant xmas gifts i could buy myself, a champagne cork flew out of my imagination and into the room, ricocheting off the rothko i'd just bought.

with my good hand – the one not flailing like a firehose, spurting oil, coating every surface of the room – i caught that champagne cork and stopped up the hole.

i felt the oil coursing thru me. my arm buzzed all night with bubbling crude.

i jolted bolt upright in the middle of the night with a thought: 'i need to get myself to an oil refinery'

so the next morning i sponged up the oil from my apartment carpets, put it into tupperware containers. i carried these tupperware containers down to the trains and went to the no-man's land at the other end of the DLR. out there i found some homeless people slumbering against a brick wall. i got close and realized they were trash bags.

'do you know if there's a oil refinery here?'

nothing.

'do ya?' i axed them.

the bags stared up at me like i was a idiot.

so i axed them again. this time with a real axe.

garbage blew allover the road.

in the distance were two fellows in pinstriped suits taking turns handshaking one another. as i approached they grew much taller than expected, loomed above me. and i realized then that one was a lamp post and the other one was a tree. they both appeared pinstriped because of what the seagulls had done to 'em.

i asked these fellows the same question and got the same answer … so i raised the axe above my head, ready to give hell to the tree. i swung and missed and lopped my own foot off.

i fell backwards onto my ass. clinky clonky clockwork noises came from inside my belly. i could hear them clearly cause the concave cup of my belly button acted like the horn of a tiny gramophone. cer-ching, cer-ching, cer-ching, coming up from inside me. cer-ching, cer-ching, like a cash register. i felt my leg stiffen like a pipe … and a torrent of pound coins came firing out of my leg. i was shooting money out into the world, a gatling gun of wealth, not warfare.

the coins jangled off the lamp post and a couple of particularly high flying ones knocked seagulls out of the sky. serves 'em right for pinstriping everything will nilly. pinstripes aren't in fashion anymore. and ones that smell like THAT have never been in fashion.

some coins rolled toward me and i could see from their shine they were brand spanking new. it's then that i realised the hole in my leg was a mouth of the mint. nothing fresher than a mouth of the mint!

'my leg hole!' i cried to the empty road. 'is a mouth of the mint! we're all rich!'

well, hearing that the road didn't stay empty for long. people emerged from doors and windows and cracks in the street. they ran into the showering coins like harlem kids playing in a fire hydrant in the heat of july. they danced for exactly the length of a coca cola commercial before they started squabbling and streetfighting eachother – shoving eachother outta the way, uppercutting eachother, poking one anothers eyes out, each trying to collect as much money as possible from the gutters and drains.

'i'm rich, i'm rich' one fatass said as an elderly babe broke an umbrella over his noodle.

they lined up to fill buckets and suitcases from the hole in my
leg. one opportunistic mama backed the trunk of her car up,
then the bed of a truck, then two transit vans, 6 wheelbarrows
and a child's red painted wagon. before long there was a line of
traffic like rushhour offa manhattan. or like the line of cars into
the drive-in movie the first time they showed deep throat.
'enough is enough' i said after hrs of this.
the crowd groaned at first but they knew i had a point. one
person used their jumper cables to heat up the flesh of my leg
and melt it, closing the wound shut. sealing off the mouth of the
mint.
as i clambered to my feet balanced on the shoulders of strangers,
a child handed me my foot … the wind had blown it 2 blocks
down, the child had pulled it sopping from the soggy jaws of the
family dog.

i took the DLR home with tubs of oil under one arm, my foot
tucked up under the other. i hobbled from lewisham station to
my house. i opened my door. then i opened a can of spaghetti-
O's. then i ate all those Os in front of grand designs … they were
re-upholstering some guys uterus. hoping to knock a wall down.
give it that open, airy feeling. dig up the back yard and lay down
an in-ground colostomy bag. strip off this 1970s wallpaper, why
not install some underfloor heating straight into the pelvic floor?
ya know, usual TV fayre.
i felt a little groan from 'downstairs' of my own. so i visited the
little boys room. i squeezed out a long hot shit, thinking 'i hate
it when people say little boys room … i hate it so much that i
think i hate everyone who has ever said it. it's both flirtatious
and infantile. the only excuse for talking like that is if you are a
pedophile *and* a coprophiliac … if you are willing to admit that
you are both those things. not one. not the other. both. then
and only then, can you call the crapper the little. boys. room.' i
squeezed off the end of the terd and wiped …
scape scrape scrape said the paper to my ass.
i tilted & squinted in the low, dingy light. i had to: i was trying to
see what had transferred onto the paper. maybe i was mistaken
but it seemed to me that my feces was bubbly and ink black. not
my usual product. normally it's coffee grounds straight thru, like

i'd opened up the french press, clamped it between my cheeks and done a headstand … or else it's like a tree branch in autumn … dry and hard and curly-clawed, expect kinda rubbery cause it's mostly made out of mozarella cheese, hot sauce and haribo. but this. wasn't that.

it looked like sludgy rabbit pellets, looked black at first but had a deep red tinge like guiness.

i brought the toilet paper up to my nose.

sniff.

sniff.

  … sniff.

i had a hunch. but i had to taste it to be sure.

i closed my eyes and stuck out my tongue. and guess what?

i was shitting beluga caviar!

FLASHBACK TO THE PRESENT

i approach you in a movie theatre. you sit comfy. reclined, lumbar region relaxing into the fabric of your seat. eyes glued to the screen. the glue is … metaphorical. celluloid flickers, electric fire, it's a digital print but you know what i mean, dust storms swirl in the projector beam, it whirs if only you could hear it under the soundtrack, swirling jazz or haunting orchestral music, the sound of the past, the sound of not anymore. popcorn is a buttery smudge in your crotch. maybe you're here on a date. or maybe you prefer to come alone. it's just simpler that way. tonight, i enter the theatre. i see the back of your head, shadowy silhouette of your hair-do against the bright white light of the screen, projection beam. i sidestep down the aisle behind your aisle. excuse me, excuse me, excuse me. the place is almost empty cause there's a million ways to be distracted, a million ways to be entertained. top pix, net flix, rock hard nine inch … i stop right behind you, inches behind you. you sense me closing in. as i kneel to whisper and blow bologna breath in your ear. i press these wet lips to the back of your neck. a love bite. a hickey. ok, a bruise. not love precisely. a lust bite. i say: *don't turn around. don't look behind you. you don't know me. i'm a stranger. i could be anyone.* i tell myself that in my hopeless desperate coiling rope just in case moments. i tell myself: i could be *anyone.* … your eyes are glued to the screen, pupils dilate. the glue is no longer metaphorical. the glue is real. take your eyes off the screen, take your eyes off the reel to reel, take your eyes off the screen, the glue is real. you are glued to the unreal. and even it. is too real. i am coiling rope around your neck. i am pulling it taut against your throat. i am, yeah, throttling you. throttling you with your own intestine.   … i am a killer in a movie theatre. i am your killer in a movie theatre.

after you're gone.

a thick film of who gives a shit coats everything.
your ghost is a smudge you leave on this world.
before during & after

i kill you.

i drop your body into a trash compactor. you are stripped of all your recyclable parts. anything that can be reduced, reused or recycled is. the rest is crushed down, boiled and buried in the city landfill.

you rest forever in the dump.

AFTER THE MURDER

when they do your autopsy they have to undo what i've done to you to figure out what i've done to you.

autopsy photographs, hot snaps of your cold body, are a hit on the blackmarket mail order circuit. i order a set myself, to cover my tracks. never suspect me now will they?

you are in a morgue, laying supine on a drainage table. i have gotten away with it again.

in a deadend small-town just north of hell.

cathode waits for her boyfriend to come back from the bathroom.

she suspects he's jerking off in there but he's actually throwing up

boyfriend walks back out into the restaurant and it's easier to feign guilt like a chronic pork puller than to admit he hates his fucking body

he wants to drop a dress size,

and besides,

he's gotta get down to the lower weight class in karate this winter so he can be the big fist in the small pond rather than come home dalmation skinned with blood blisters for being the fat kids whipping boy. cause every fighter knows the lightest heavy weight don't stand a chance. come hellfire n high water, the lighter of 2 heavy metals got more commercial potential.

cathode stares out the window, wonders why he don't fuck her like he used to,

a slice of untouched key lime pie sits idly on the table between them.

she thinks 'damn, you know how many boys in this town would be lining up to kill an hour sweating on me! or girls … if i knew where to find 'em …'

petit does she realize it's nothing to do with perfect her. it's the thought of himself naked, fat and gyrating. it's enough to spin him out suicidal for days.

she resolves to read some sex tips in cosmo, try and tempt him away from his hand – and to cut down on pie … if that's what it takes to salvage the relationship.

she breathes a (huff) and slides the plate towards him like a peace offering.

the waitress brings the cheque.

the key lime pie stares up at the boyfriend, with that taunting look in its tiny key lime eyes …

I KINDA REMEMBER THE SPERM I WAS

i remember thinking 'it's hard to believe this is the best we have to offer. i am not natural selection at its finest. if nature were trying to slow the proliferation of the human species it might start sending duds like me down the pipes. oh sure, why don't you impregnate the egg, weasel? ... let's see how mighty and long living the human species is, how much more damage they can do with your emaciated, scrawny, pink n transparent, tired all the time, good for nothing, alcoholic, irish genes off the bench and on the playing field.' whoops. and then i got kicked outta the plane and started my descent to this planet, and if nature'd had her way i'd have crash landed at the starting gate, but medicine caught me before i expired and reeled my ass in like a dead shark in a fishing net, cause every life is a fucking miracle. and every life is sacred. and guess what? i been happy to be alive every goddamn second since.

thoughts after *COME TO DADDY*

we play baseball on a 🪂 in the rust
the ball is the 🩶 you tore out of daddy

a 🩶 made of naked ambition
& clothed lust.

come
come
come
come
come to daddy

come
come
come
come
come for daddy.

SPEEDWAY

*2033,
location unknown*

it was a nice day at the speedway. out beyond the city limits where one county meets another county. 12 bars from nowhere as the crow flies. where the speed freaks and adrenaline junkies come to come and die. one by one by engine fire, by petroleum fumes and burning tires. one by one the adrenaline junkies come to the speedway to die.

'but who wants to go out with a full deck?' they think. 'just one last bolt of adrenaline. just one more race.' forever chasing that first ever high.

when they made motors illegal they pushed it underground. it happens in secret now, way out past the edge of town. camouflaged security patrol the perimeter. hardly any fans, hardcore fetishists only. purely a purist's purist pursuit.

ladies n gentleman, boys and girls, cocks n balls n ball bags n ball busters, shemales with injun headdresses like feather dusters. conditions are right and the danger is real, it's hot on the tarmac tonight, the checker flag flies like a chessboard made of fabric, bleets the tannoy.

RRMM RRMM RRMM RRRMMM, say the engines, as the speed kings and speed queens line up and vy for poll position.

'the death toll is high man, and so am i.' cooter pink is fidgeting nervously in the grandstands with casts on two broken legs. she is a chalice lipped vixen. was born the son of a boxer, now she's the daughter of a deadman. one too many seasons as daddy's punchbag and daddy met the devil. she used her inheritance to mould the world into one she could live in, mould herself into someone she could live with. and if you think cooter pink has taken one single jab from any fist since … ? you'd better think again. you'd be safer thinking about something else …

'pedal down' she cries, 'pushed into the seat back no airbag
in front of me, cause if i'm dying by impalement on a steering
column tonight i'm doing it under a freeman's moon.' she is
quoting the driver's oath, spoken at induction and then again at
every race: 'and if i'm dying i'm doing it on my time, my way,
and not a moment too ...'

she is saying this for the benefit of the newbie who drove her
here: randi rush. she's a waitress at cooter's drinking hole, and
she makes big tips, the biggest. she has diamonds where other
people have roughage, and vice versa. randi cracks her knuckles
and rolls a cigarette in one smooth motion. cooter screams
'come on!' as if that will start the race. the engines growl as if to
say 'we were born ready don't blame us'

the officials and mechanics and flagmen – flaggots cooter calls
'em – are still holding a huddle. cooter screams again to impress
randi. it kinda works. randi hands her the cig, cooter laments it
ain't grass, her eyes turn furtive n she admits there's nitrogen in
her bloodstream, took a hit at breakfast and it still ain't worn off.
has a teensy weensy bit left, does randi wants some to take the
edge off? ... a trickle of red streams all 4 nostrils. cooter recounts
to randi for the 24th time her tale of flipping a flaming
wreck, explains she'll be back on the track the minute she's out
of her goddamn leg casts.

not long now racefans, just the final checks from the marshals?
randi sits forward and her pupils dilate.
and they'reeeee OFFF!!

*first pedal down and the wunderkid pulls out, makes a break for the
jackknife, but oh no it won't be that easy, as the italian stallion defends
his position on greasy wheels, who's bolting for the exit, snaking back n
forth looking for an opening and he gets it, he seizes it? but what? the
prom queen in 88 will not let it happen, she's boxing him out driving
a very wide car indeed. and he's spinning off into the sandbox, twisted
metal cage into the tire wall already, that had to hurt, and the front
runners are pulling away from the pack, a grease slick as carmine in
kitkar 669 skids napalm death streak out of his muffler, laying a liquid
trap for those behind him, one car spins out, another car spins out, oh
god, you better hope there's free beds at the morgue tonight cause we're
gonna need 'em!, and penelope clit-stop is coming up pretty in the
pink car behind rodruiguez deplores, (sidebar: rodruiguez deplores is*

still wanted in mehi-ko for a wrap sheet so long it'd make your sister blush!) and what's this? what's this? they're bumper to bumper, grill to grill in a love grip that's destined to kill. deprlores, the mehi-mobile is crushed like a doctor pepper can in a trash compactor but he's somehow alive, pulling his body from the wreckage, gasping for air, and what now? what now? what now? deplores is … approaching the other crashed car, number 23, number 23 which is fully aflame folks, soon to be cinders. and he's reaching into this bonfire to? to? to pull out the other driver. and hug her in what looks like more than a platonic love embrace, he's shattered the glass of her helmet for one last look into her dying eyes, he's dousing and bedabbling her charred remains with sweat from his lusty latin brow. and what's this? what's this? he's stomping on her dead chest now like it's a bellows, using the air left in her body to blow out the fire that's engulfing her racecar? he's stepping into her motorcar, strapping in, and what? what? re-entering the race? ladies and gentleman he's back on the speedway, the lusty latin number 74 has hijacked car 23, he is driving his dead ride's ride, and is not to be out done tonight. meanwhile at turn six it's wheel bars on twin cars, locked in spaghetti abandon, spinning t-junction like a cyclone made of hot steel. she's jamming her gearbox and sputtering purple smoke into the kentucky fried sky. with hi jinx like this there'll be more than a few babies conceived in the grandstands tonight! this is a gunshow and what more do ya know!

15 finish the race, barely alive. and in this league they all get medals. just for surviving. just for having the baloney to finish the race.

the sun sets like an orange peel on a tie-dye sky, each racer stands holding their battered face up for judgement, limbs missing, the occasional eyeball swinging from the socket. nothing that can't be repaired. nothing they can't learn to live without. bloodspattered wrecks sit cooling in the frozen sun. each one a unique work of auto-destructive art. petrol go-go machines, kit cars, junk heaps. rubber, metal and fibreglass chassis. mixed media collage.

and they wear battlescars and broken blood vessels with pride. shoulder to fractured shoulder, self-made monsters, frankensteining themselves, removing themselves from this world … one unnecessary bodypart at a time.

the tiny but ecstatic crowd clap until their hands bleed and whistle til the tips of their whistling fingers are pruned like after bathtime.

cooter smashes a beer bottle in approval, she uses the broken glass to comb her orange mullet. randi and cooter both apply clementine lipstick, passing it back n forth like a joint. randi says i'll be right back. gets up to go to the bar. adrenaline from her first taste of daredevil driving courses thru her, her cheeks are flushing red round. randi has that *glow*, kinda like the one breeding people like to point out when they notice it on eachothers preggo face. 'pregnancy's stupid' randi thinks, imagining how hard it would be to give up drinking for 9 days, let alone months, 'goddamn' she thinks, finally getting why cooter never shuts the hell up about renegade stunt car racing.

back when the speedway was open legally there were 35 kiosks selling beer. and about 2 dozen hotdog stands. now there's only one bar and it's stocked with lukewarm low percent dogpiss. randi joins the back of the line, feeling in her leather pants for a 5 … if that ain't enough for a couple lousy beers in this fucking place she'll turn on the charm. either that or she'll turn off the charm, pull the blade from her belt and rob the joint. either way, she won't go thirsty.

cooter is in the grandstands. the drugs are wearing off, she is becoming more herself, that is to say more the version of herself that other people recognize, that other people like, that other people tolerate. she bites her nails and applies lipstick. she thinks about all the ways she's gonna do and be done by randi that night. or so she hopes. or so she hopes randi hopes. surely this tension isn't just in her head?

YEOOOWWWOOOO – a siren cuts the night, tranquility dies a death in the grandstands!

the remaining few fans duck for cover, 'not this shit again' one
old timer cries, – bang bang bang bang bang – shots are fired
in the distance, machinegun blasts – rat-a-tat rat-a-tat-tat-tat- rat-
a-tat – one of the incognito guards lets off a solar flare from the
watchout … is fizzes and fumes in the sky. this indicates the
direction the narcs are rolling in from … this time it's north. due
north.

the marshalls panic. mechanics start running out of the pits, they
take up wrenches and tire irons like weaponry, ready to hurl
them overhand if necessary.

sirens are cutting the night, sirens are getting closer and closer,
the racers jump in their petrol cars, passengers pile in, the cars
sputter and growl and speed off one by one in twelve different
directions. the smart ones drive south, away from the interlopers.
the idiot ones drive north, straight into the commotion.

the few fans left abandon the grandstands, scattering in every
direction, running for cover in the woods, jumping ditches,
crossing the old sandpits, running out towards the highway to
hitchhike home. making a break on foot, a marshall kicks the
door open to a security hut and flips random switches on a
generator. she is trying to power the whole thing down … as if
the cops would fall for that at this point. too little. too late. too
stupid an idea.

when the cops roll in everywhere within eyeshot is abandoned
… only cooter in her casts is left behind. she screamed for help
but no one heard her. cooter's never been caught by the pigs
before. in three prior raids she'd gunned off in her motor. but
with her legs in casts cooter can't even take her chances on foot.
cooter doesn't wanna be caught by the pigs. so she listens to the
sirens. and the sound of the cop cars: the hum of their efficient
electric engines is effeminate and high pitched, sounds like
they're surfing in on sewing machines. even the *sound* makes her
angry.

she pictures herself spitting in the face of a cop. she pictures her
ass in jail. chicks like her don't fare well in jail. cooter ducks for
cover between two rows of seats, lays low, lays real low, lays as
low as she can lay … low.

cooter don't believe in god,
but cooter starts to pray.

...

scattered after the police raid dufff durango found himself holed
up in the same abandoned meat locker as usual. industrial
fridges and cold tile, sun streaming in through boarded up
windows. grease browned ceiling and dusty meat hooks hanging.
when the speedway was open this had been the remotest hotdog
stand. now it was a derelict clapboard shack, no good for
nothing except for laying low during a police raid.
dufff flipped a breaker, surprised to find the electricity still
worked ... the lights buzzed on, the radio blared a familiar song,
cut thru with sirens and air raid alarms. (byooo – byooo)
dufff scavenged for something to eat. racing is hungry work.
deepfat fryers rusted over and out of use. fridges unplugged. a
rota still pushpinned to the wall. marianella had worked a lot
of shifts the week the racetrack closed. alejandro's name was
scored thru in red ink. guess he got pinched in the downsize.
maybe he had a shitty work ethic. no doubt exacerbated by the
fact his name was spelled wrong on the rota. allah-jam-donut.
as in praise be. to krispy kreme. maybe this was an affectionate
nickname cause he was carrying extra pounds. maybe it was an
honest mistake. maybe it was bullying. either way, alejandro
didn't see the funny side and he sure didn't high tail it outta bed
to get to work on time.
dufff found an old jar of mayonnaise and scooped it dry with
his hands, sucking the mayo off his fingers, pretending they was
spoons. he heard the creek of the back door opening and the
clack clack clack of boots on tin. someone else had found his
hideout. busted.

dufff wiped the mayo onto his jeans and fumbled with his gun, 'who the fuck?' he thought.

she rounded the corner, expecting to find the place abandoned. square black hair and heartshaped features, eyes wide like a hunted animal when she spotted him. she pulled her knife from her belt. he moved fast like a hunter, disarmed her swift, knife clattering to the dusty floor. he flattened her against the meatlocker door and pushed his barrel chest against her squishy tits, pinning her, he a woodchipped beheamouth with a beard made of scars. her, buttery pancake batter sloshing out of leather.

'who the fuck?' he said aloud. he put the gun to her head.

'your wettest nightmare by the looks of things …' she held his stare. his equal, his match. or the flame that would engulf it.

he panted and cocked the pistol. 'are you completely unafraid of me?'

'i like your driving' she said 'but you need to work on your hair-pin turns. that's where you're losing ground.'

he cocked the pistol again. if that's even possible.

'i'm just a race fan' she said. 'i ain't no expert.'

'you ain't a cop?'

'do i look like a cop?'

his eyes drank the pancake batter, and licked the frying pan clean.

'you look …' he searched inside himself for the perfect words, 'you look like … a good dream on a bad night.'

she parted her lips slowly, a web of saliva stretched from the bottom lip to the top. two orange lips like clementine peels. she pierced the salival web with the tip of her tongue, cherry red and drug dry. she closed her eyes in slow motion: eye lashes long like a tolstoy book and stiff like broom bristles.

he uncocked the pistol. … twice.

she pushed past him and made herself comfortable on a stack of old cardboard boxes. the side of the boxes had hotdogs with faces. the faces were smiling, happy cause the hotdogs had hands in which they gripped smaller hotdogs. hotdogs eat their young, randi guessed.

'you gonna give me a ride back into town? you gonna give me a ride back to my car?'

dufff didn't answer.

'you gonna give me a ride in the back seat of my car?'

dufff didn't answer some more.

'i practically crawled here from the grandstands on both knees.' she said.

'why didn't ya crawl on just one knee?'

she gave him the finger. and then the other finger.

'it ain't safe to leave. we make a fortification here' he grumbled.

'how long til it's gonna be safe?' she said. 'i work a shift tomorrow morning'

'should be safe by morning. what time's your shift?'

'2pm.'

'that ain't morning'

'it is in my trade'

'what's yer trade?'

'booze. got any?'

he shook his head: no.

she looked around. 'well then what good are ya?'

'driving is all i'm good for. i'm a one trick pony who's hung like a horse.'

he felt stupid for saying that immediately. but it was the truth.

'tonight was my first race.' randi said, 'i like watching things and this was at least as good as watching microsoft paint dry.'

dufff opened the old coke fridge to be sure there was nothing to drink in there. the old coke fridge hadn't been plugged in for ten years. it was empty except for spiders. he slammed the fridge door shut. why did the door need to be shut if it was unplugged? habit he guessed. what's a refrigerator when it's not refrigerating anything? just an ugly closet.

'what the hell's yer name, anyway?'

'anyway's my name. good guess.'

he pointed the gun at her. dufff hated sarcasm. randi's heart started to visibly beat in her chest.

'randi' randi said. 'my name is randi rush. it's the name my parents gave me and i've used it ever since.'

she didn't ask him his name because she didn't care. she had no memory for shit like that. what she did know was that his car was called 79 and he was a hell of a driver. he put the gun away. a minute passed. and then another minute passed. and then two more. and then all those minutes passed away.

'there's gotta be something to drink round here' randi wiggled across the room, kicked open the pantry door. he smelled her perfume as she passed – at least he thought it was her perfume, it was actually a spritz of cooter's – *date rape* by calvin klein.

randi ransacked the pantry. condiments and mouldy boxes thrown over creamy shoulders.

'yer first race … eh randi? so yer a virgin?'

she didn't answer. he felt embarrassed that he'd said that.

'yeah, maybe' she said '… that would explain the cherry splatter between my thighs.'

she came outta the pantry with a rusty metal can. 'either that or i cut myself shaving!'

he smirked and sparked a cuban. brown smoke coughed in his red raw throat.

she takes a long slurp from a kerosene canister. lifts that gas can right to her lips. lipstick comes smudging off onto the rim. now he knows she means business. she gulps down that lighter fluid, feels it strip her insides of all that's still alive, hawks it back up and spits it out in an elegant jet. he ducks. the stream hits the end of his tightly rolled cigar, making a flamethrower like the climax of a kiss concert.

'hell' she thinks. 'don't we make a heavenly pair.'

and she pounces on him, straddles him up against the sink. he smiles like a hangdog and blows cuba fumes into her eyes. she holds his stare, and parts those puckering clementines.

'i like the glow of your habitus. you sure got a bright disease alright.'

they touch tongues, electric, eyes open to drink in the moment, none of that romance shit. this is lust. she can feel the heat coming off him, she can feel him closing in, he tastes the gasoline on her tongue as he drinks her saliva, she can feel him straining against his denim. hands fidgeting up and down her spine, nothing better than a strong man going weak, she blows hot air into his mouth, he swallows it, lets her fill his lungs, tongues flapping against eachother, like leathery snakes, she breaks the kiss, and leans back. she raises one arms up above her head, winds back and karate chops him in his chest, just hard enough to sting. he throws her backwards onto the stack of cardboard boxes, she hurls a hotdog box back at him in defense, he ducks it and pulls the gun. the happy hotdog chokes and dies trying to swallow a chunk of his own son.

dufff levels the pistol at randi.

they pant.

she crawls towards him on all fours, offers her throat. he clears his (gulp) and raises his pistol to her face. runs its barrel sleek along her cheeks, she puffs her cheeks out she puffs them in she puffs them out she puffs them, heartshaped rosy red features, she puts her hands behind her head in surrender. she darts her tongue out slow. takes it for a sloppy walk along her bottom lip … and feeds her tongue tip, cherry red, into the open barrel of the gun, plugging up the muzzle.

she looks up at him and they hold eye contact.

they listen to eachother panting like it's music.

they listen to eachother panting.

it is music.

the blood is pounding in his temples, his mouth is dry, his legs wobbling. the room smells like animals in panic. like the in-tray at a slaughterhouse.

there's a new twinkle in her poker player stare. she bats those eyelids again, broom bristles sweeping her face. one of her arms moves down her body, across her thigh, surely, surely, surely up inside her. her hears a squelching sound faint but distinct. she holds his stare, her mouth falls open a bit, saliva bubbles at the corners, she is rapid finger self service check out check out check out check it out check mate machining herself. he widens his eyes in disbelief, blinks twice, and his gaze drifts towards her crotch to verify what his nostrils already know.

the minute eye contact is broken her free arm swipes down in a judo motion, and twists the pistol from his grip. she's on her feet in no time, sucking moisture off her fingers like colonel sanders' secret recipe. she kicks him in the chest, he clatters against the coke fridge. she holds the pistol, limp wristed like a pro. he raises his arms like 'ya got me'. she hocks up a loogie and spits out a huge gob of mucus and gasoline residue. it splatters his face. 'don't. wipe. clean' she instructs. he listens, he does as he's told. the loogie cools as he does exactly what she says ... he follows instructions well:

he opens his jeans and shows her what he's got. his thing is brittle like treebark and dark red like beetroot, it's 14 inches long and 6 inches across. *is this all you've got?* she thinks, not the best she's seen but she's seen alot. *well, he's one hell of a driver.*

she holds him at gunpoint while he puts on a show, he jerks it fast and then he jerks it slow.

'show me how ya do it when nobody's watching' she goads.

'i never practice, i ain't an amateur'

she picks the remainder of his cuban up from the floor and relights it. she pushes the point, demands to see what nobody sees. he licks one of his mayonnaise fingers, widens his stance and shoves it into his rectum. the rectal canal beads a pus thing to lube it up a little. he starts himself kinda slow back there but gains momentum, working soft circles, and then inserts a second finger, working himself in tandem motions, long slow strokes down the 14 incher, tight fast circles in the back ... it takes a bit of practice but it's just the x-rated version of the rub yer stomach & pat yer head routine. which goes pretty well so long as ya don't think too much about it.

randi rush peels her leathers away, and out spurts her body. she is a fertility goddess carved in butter. dufff's peepers drink her in. her pot belly, her tangled tufts of wild black pubic hair, her wafer thin pink of untidy labia curling from her crotch crack as if to say please please it's lonely in here! little old me in this big big house! origami folds that spell cu-cu-cu-cum hither, then white thighs like a storm warning, kneecaps cut n scraped like a toddlers, faint black stubble down her shins, ankles more pornographic than your whole body, oddly square feet, a heartshaped tattoo on the top of one, 'what's the tattoo?' he asks. she doesn't answer but while he's staring at her feet, a single drop of moisture falls from her trembling labia, *splat*, onto the top of her foot, coating the tat, varnishing it, her legs are quivering, she is knock kneed, she brings the gun up, bicep flexing, arm crooked into a right angle, she holds the gun to her own head, her other arm rises in celebration, fingers splay and run through her hair, eyes wide open, none of that romance shit, hairs bristle on her neck, her mouth drops, jaw unlocked, hot mouth superwide, she is demonstrating to him just *how* unlocked this jaw goes, she cocks the pistol, her pot belly swells in and out, her breasts, heavy and wide set, both bedaubed with axle grease, her nipples hard and dark and caked with dried mud, she lifts one tit with her free hand, squeezes, and it lactates just a little, 'don't worry' she says 'i'm not pregnant. it's backed up cum.'

'your cum?' dufff asks. 'or the last guys?'

she licks the glistening white from her nipple and releases the tit, letting it slap heavy against her ribcage. she orders him to turn around, he says no, he refuses to take his eyes off her. it's not clear whether it's lust or he doesn't trust her with the pistol. both? 'your choice' she says, motioning for him to put one leg up on the nearby sink. to splay himself. his hairy kneecap cracks as he bends it. he contorts into the position she demands. his balls hang low, like boulders swinging from a rubberband. his chest heaves beneath his shirt, his nipples razor thru the fabric, slicing holes in his shirt. her nipples respond by puckering and lactating. his arms are like brick cylinders with unfortunate tattoos on 'em. veins visible inside biceps. she gets down on the floor and buttscoots towards him, gun pointed upwards. he is braced, one leg on the sink, everything exposed. she gets as close as she can to his everything, studies his perineum like a medical student would. his heart is beating so loud she can hear it. he begins to work his 14 inches again. slow rhythms, hanging on for dear life with both hands. ... that's 7 inches per hand! his heart is beating audibly – thud-thud-thud-thud-thud – because he knows what's coming ...

she spits on the tip of the gun and feeds it *into* him, works it with crescent motions and shallow thrusts, pushes the whole length of the barrel into him. up to the fingerguard, and back down again, up to the fingerguard and back down again, moisture smearing the barrel, he moans low and long, unnnnghhh, hands like lightning on his 14 inches now, mouth open perfect circle like he's catching ping pong balls, spit falls to grease the lightning, one handed, his freehand limp fingers find his own chest, tweezes nipple, cuts thumb on the razor, blood spurts, he lets go of the cock and it seesaws wildly from the base, like when ya twang a ruler off the side of a desk, doy-yoy-yoy-yoy-yoy-yoy-yoy-yoy-yoy

'don't blow it, don't blow it, don't let go' she cries. he grips himself again, squeezes his eyes shut, engages the kegel muscles and a million baseball statistics hurl across his mind's eye.

his breathing slows as he steadies himself on the sink. his breathing slows and she fucks him with the gun. slowly, then less slowly, then not slowly at all. she watches his anus take the metal, she watches it drink the metal in, she watches it throb and pucker, the hungry little thing. a pool of her is forming at her feet, she squats with her knees together, origami soaked n squished, her toes are sticky in the pooling liquid, like changing room at the swimming pool, her thighs are pressed together crushing her throbbing origami, liquid gushing out, soaking all of the folds, she works the gun faster and faster, she dribbles from herself like an open faucet. the speed of the gun thrusts seem to control, scratch that, do control the jelly in her juicebox.

she pulls the gun out and transfers it to the other hand, sore wrist, rsi if you're not careful, his back hole is a sopping mess, the anal lips are puckered and pimpled, his ass is left hanging open ... she takes a draw on the cigar stub. grits it in her teeth.

and a devilish thought comes over her … devilish indeed, a thought straight from the pits of hell.

she balances the cigar stub on the tip of her finger, and feeds the cigar stub up *into* him, pushing it as far inside as she can. he feels the hot embers of the still lit cigar, and the rough of its paper wrapping, the chemical rush of nicotine jacking off straight into his mainframe as the foreign object lodges itself against his most sensitive membranes.

once the stub is in as far as she can voyage with her longest finger, she pulls the finger out slowly, licks the moisture from it, and seals his butt closed. with a kiss.

he is drunk with a kind of pain/pleasure now, as he lowers his leg off the sink and tumbles down the coke fridge door, as he slides down to the floor. she squats over his face, peels herself open *(saliva noise)*

frostbitten nipples buttery thighs stale breath and a fresh lust freezedried for just such an occasion oh yeah she was hot to trot and trot she would like a pig on cloven high heel hoofs. he goes down on her like a tsunami hitting a shoreline all wet spray and no particular aim, tourists running for cover in a tuft of pubic hair like palm trees, her outer labia quivering like an infant's mouth an inch from a nipple. randi rush is a chick so mean she could curl all 6 of her lips.

she squats over him, devouring his face with her wound. she feels lust buzz like electric current, her inner skins bristling.
'how many licks does it take to get to the centre of the tootsie roll?' he asks coming up for air.
'55' she says 'if you do it right'
she holds the gun to his temple and instructs, exactly. how. she. needs. needs. needs.
'do this. like this. and do that. exactly. there. and exactly. then. and exactly. now.'
he works it, 'faster. faster. and not so hard. and down a bit, and under. under.' he works it like his tongue is double jointed. high school spanish starts flooding back to him. so he conjugates

some verbs up into her. he quotes the trickiest passages of hamlet, she cries. she cries. 'under. under. under.' he scrapes the tip of his tongue against the underside of her clitoris until he feels it pulsing and bulging and extending out of her like a number 2 pencil. from pink to red to purple to black, he licks the fat pad of his thumb and works it with that, like he's giving the thumbs up to god, she presses her throbbing calamari against his mouth, it elasticates open, swallowing the bottom half of his face, he does a prose poem about pirates, she starts burbling like a cauldron, steam shoots out, scalding his skin with second degree burns but he doesn't care. what's a few more scars on a face like his. he counts down the last 15 licks of the tootsie roll, screaming up into her like a drill seargant, 14-13-12, and by then he's really got the hang, she leans back like she's rodeo riding a bull, both feet lift off the ground, 7-6 he flexes his tongue and lifts her up with it, her matte black pubic tufts are a soggy blur, 3-2-1 tremors and tidal waves and tributaries are blown open, *liftoff.* a biblical gush, and thighs like a thunderclap for 4 minutes an electrical storm in a styrofoam t cup, she raises her arms in celebration, losing herself to the moment, eyes rolled back like a sarcastic epileptic, drool cascading the mouth, her feet flex and point flex and point flex and point wildly like an electrocuted ballerina, like somebody just dropped a hair dryer into the swan lake, her hands go all palsied and she accidentally squeezes the gun trigger.

a deaf-making bang from the thundering gun as it shakes the shit outta the little shack.
the bullet blows a hole in the wall of the hot dog stand.
a pane of old plate glass rattles out of a frame, klatter and kshhh to the floor.

she trembles, and slops off of him, curls fetal.

he falls back and pants, staring at the cobwebbed ceiling, that old familiar cobwebbed feeling, a little high from the asphyxiation.

their ears are ringing from the gun blast. eachother's panting is music. music that fades out. fades out to biblical hush.

...

the shot was heard a mile away. the shot was heard by all the cops within that mile too. they radio'd eachother frantically asking who done shot the shot, who done heard the shot, who done reckoned they was closest to it.

detective kim rex was part of the squad by the grandstands. she'd arrested the cowering fucker in the security hut, hugging the generator for heat, the cowering idiot who tried to power the whole thing down. rex read that fool her rights, though in truth she didn't have none. petrol burning was a serious crime in the year 2033, worse than rape and murder combined, a petrol criminal was about as welcome on planet earth then as a pederast blowing loads on a zygote would be today.
sub human. sub animal. barely scraping vegetable.

one of rex's men was scouring the grandstands, flashlight in hand, shining the beam up and down the rows of seats, mostly cardboard soda boxes and prehistoric beerfart stains on wood benches, rickety shelter half beaten by the wind, remnants of glory days of yore, of a barbaric sport that didn't happen round these parts much anymore. in the 2020's public opinion had turned against any pursuits physically dangerous to human beings, and any pursuits dangerous to the environment – so a sport like renegade motorcar driving, lethal to both, was *doubly* out of fashion.
the grandstands were crumbling and 'thank god' thought the cop. his flashlight lit up ancient signage advertising a muffler brand long outta business, faded from the sun and rotten from the rain. the cop heard a rustle or a whimper or some such human sound so shined his light directly at a lump of fear in the

trembling darkness. a fear that he didn't yet know was cooter pink.

cooter's legs ached and itched in their casts. she was dying to scream. or talk. or fight. or something. she had been lying as still as she could, trying not to hyperventilate, trying not to sneeze, trying not to do any goddamn thing ... and for a drug addict with adhd, that was like playing piano in gloves made of concrete.

the beam of the flashlight swished across her vision, the steps got closer. her spine stiffened. cop boots crunched rubber soles on ancient wood. the grandstand swayed gently in the night breeze. cooter's mind raced: she figured that if it was just one cop alone she could kiss him then kill him. she licked her lips for the kiss and fumbled around in her pockets for a weapon. a lighter. lipstick. bubblegum. she figured if it was two cops or more she'd probs need a better weapon than bubblegum ... she'd once ripped the adam's apple right out of a man's haranguing throat, but that was before her driving days, before she had a healthy outlet for her rage. and back then she pretty much took amphetamines all day like it was her job.

the boots crunched again. one. row. away. now.

right *then* is when the gunshot was heard. the cop spun to face the direction of the blast, the south east side of the speedway. he clicked his flashlight off and sprinted down the rickety stairs of the old grandstand. he took the bottom ten steps in one leap, twisting and spraining his ankle at the bottom. 'goddamnit' he cursed. cooter spied him through a crack in the seats. nothing much to look at, she thought. nothing much to listen to either. his voice sounded like a piss balloon. he cursed the lord again: 'goddamnit'.

cooter, however, was now *thanking* that very same lord. a lord who she all of a sudden kinda-sorta believed in. she strained her ears and heard pigs hollering at eachother, squealing like the sandwich fillings they were.

the ladycop had a shaven head and weathered face, laugh lines like napkin creases at her mouth n eyes, looked like an ageing punk, tough like a DC hardcore singer. but she spoke with a bubbly demeanor, big eyes, animate features like a children's tv star. even at 100 yards away cooter could see that she had *huge* tearducts. all the other pigs seemed to respect her. they certainly listened when she spoke.

cooter heard the cop with the sprained ankle report the grandstands was 'all clear' … 'ha' she thought. 'ha'.

ladycop asked if he was 'double sure' and he said 'triple ma'am'. he was gunning to be where the action was. he was gunning to use his gun. & he was getting sloppy. cooter watched them pile into their cruisers. battery powered cop cars. electric engines idling on standby. three cop cars peeled away one after one after one.

the wind shook the grandstand gently. the electric engines disappeared into the distance. making hardly any sound. making hardly any smell.

cooter crawled along the seats, squatting as low as she could. it'd be just like them pigs to peel away and leave one behind, a pawn in a deek out. at the end of the row she swung her legs round. and sat up, still ducking. she surveyed all sides, couldn't see nothing. both legs were numb in their casts. she jiggled her thighs, tried to get the feeling back. nothing but tingles were on tap. she hobbled down the steps of the grandstand, down the hundred or so stairs, step after step after step after step.

she hobbled away from the grandstand, passed the kiosk and the outhouses. not a soul in sight. she hobbled into the woods and followed the dirt path. she cut off the dirt path, and took a shortcut towards the clearing. she followed cigarette butts like breadcrumbs. her legs ached in their casts. she hoped randi would be waiting at the clearing, she hoped randi knew her way to the secluded spot where they'd hidden the car. she pictured randi bolting when the cops turned up, pictured her making a break for the clearing and laying low. even if the cops had spotted randi, she didn't look like a typical petrol addict. she was new enough that she didn't reek of gasoline, didn't have that grease monkey look. she could feign ignorance, she could claim she was in the woods for any old reason, any old reason at all, no officer i had no idea there was an abandoned speedway out here, how nifty. good luck with your manhunt n all. cooter on the other hand … may as well have had tire tracks across her pretty face.

as she cut through the woods, dragging her casts through mud, her skeleton quivvered in her denim jacket. the drugs had worn off and now she was cold. and on the verge of a bad fucking mood. she started to wonder if randi might *not* have waited for her … she pictured randi bolting when the cops turned up, jamming her car into gear and pulling away in a panic. she pictured randi freaked out by the gunshots, cursing cooter for bringing her to the speedway. then she pictured randi leaving her for dead. they didn't really know eachother that well …
cooter came up through a ditch and hobbled out towards the clearing, scraping mud from her hands on some sycamore bark. she ducked behind a boulder and peered into the clearing … the car was there alright. and no noise or light or pig squealing.
score score and double score, she thought, *thank the lord.*

she pictured randi waiting for her in the car. excitedly hobbled towards it, thinking *this deffo proves randi digs me, right? right? it proves that whatever-this-is, it isn't just in my head.*
right?
RIGHT?
RIGHT?

cooter hobbled top speed to the car, rapped on the windows. no dice. not even a fluffy pair hanging from the rearview. she pushed her face to the window, nose bending piggy upwards, huge green eyes wide like platters … no. dice.

… cooter hated it when stuff turned out to be just in her head.

...

'good boy.' randi rush whispers, running her fingers through dufff durango's hair. they lay on the hot dog stand floor. in a cooling pool of her. his huge balls tight like ball bearings. his thing standing so stiff it'd crack ice. so straight you could use it as a level for putting up a set of shelves. it is vibrating and emitting a pitch that only bats can hear. 'little boy blue balls.' she purrs, kissing clementine lips to his forehead. he tastes of sweat and petrol. petrol sweat, petrol tears, petrol blood, petrol come. petrol come over here, lover.

he rolls over and looks at her, wideeyed in amazement. his body trembling with helpless lust. not like the lust of a grown man, but the lust of a child who's first experimenting with their body. confused, new, overwhelmed. child-like lust like 'what even is sex? is it a portal to another world? … is it a door to outerspace? to heaven? … surely it doesn't just lead to endless degrading repetitions of the same …'
dufff hadn't felt like this since he was a 9 year old ranch hand, wrapping his hairless bone in a flannel and pressing it against the hot radiator. cumming hands free into the flannel, just the heat of the radiator, the pressure of his body against it, soaking the flannel, fitting and starting a 60 second seizure of an orgasm, getting second degree burns on his thing in the process. that mighta been the start of dufff's attraction to self damage. that or being runover by a transport truck at 14.

'don't do it!' randi screamed in dufff's face. she could tell his body was close. though his mind had drifted far away. back to childhood. she didn't want him to give his orgasm to the past. or the future. she didn't want him to waste it. she wanted him to give his orgasm to the present. to the present tense … she winds back and karate chops him on jaw. he had a square jaw before, now it's a square jaw with a dent in it.

he spits a broken tooth out, back in the room.

'just … one … pump.' she says 'just one … ya hear me?' pulling him up into the sitting position. 'not even out in. got it? just in. just one … insertion. or else.' she says, producing the knife from nowhere.
she puts the blade to his throat.
'got it' he says.
she wraps her thighs around his torso and slides down him, leaving oil slicks the whole way. her folds curl to accept him, & in the slowest possible motion she inserts his full length in one narcoleptic crawl, a 14 inch rivet, advancing a ¼ inch at a time, slurp slurp, in tiny, almost imperceptible advances, slurp, hungry devouring every bump, twist and genital wart in the road, it is an erotic act of medical precision, religious commitment and freudian perversity. it is the sexual equivalent of tip toeing to the toilet when you're dressed to run a marathon. after all they'd done it was way less than the bare minimum. and it was perfect.
he has a flashback to the moment he is born. he has a flashback to sucking his thumb inside mother. he has a flashback to his father's insertion; the one that made him.
he's 12 inches swallowed, almost up to the hilt.
'this loads so big' durango thinks 'it's gonna hafta bifurcate inside her! no way a wad this thick n wide is gonna have any structural certainty whatsoever. i be lucky if i ain't making three babies with this gunge puppet!'
and with that he passed a white brick into her the size of ten thousand gall stones.
a whole hospital's worth of gall stones. an ejaculation so chunky it widened his hole. like he passed a bowling pin through a drinking straw. sloppy jap's eye all slack and stretched out. his body would never be the same.

his candied penis slurped out of her gelatinous laceration like a
haribo snake.
it coiled up and died in his lap.

she staggered to her feet and took a wide legged stance. a litre of
him poured out of her like she was emptying a bottle of bleach.
she put her hand round a huge knot of cum the size of a babies
skull. she tugged and tugged on the knot and metres of the stuff
spooled out of her thick n white like nautical rope. she used it to
perform japanese hentai bondage on him, and then they jumped
double dutch.

dufff looked down at his crotch. his body would never be the
same. his thing looked like a banana, half peeled, skin flapping
off it, and a few bites taken off the end. his body would never
ever ever ever be the same … not that it mattered, because:

they use sonar forensic ear goggles to get a position on the
bullet blast. they trace it using infrared swatches of calligraphic
radon to precisely the right position, that is to say, the inside of
the abandoned hot dog hut on the south east corner of the old
speedway. go go go. that is to say they trace the sound of the
bullet to within 10 feet of the elephantine ejaculation which just
took place.

randi and dufff don't hear the sewing machine engines til
they're two cross-stitches away. randi pricks her ears up 'what's
that?', she starts balling up her clothes, retrieves her knife from
wherever it clattered to when durango started spraying like a fire
hose.

the cops yowl through their megaphones, as they pile outta their
cruisers, they *have the place surrounded.*

'they don't know about you, randi' durango says. he suggest she makes a break for it out the back door. he suggest he hang his ass out the front door, turn himself in.

the cops wait the legal minimum: 3-2-1 ... and then they fill the place full of bullets. machineguns from all sides, rat-a-tat rat-a-tat rat-a-tat-tat-tat-tat, the hotdog stand is barely stand-ing by the time it's over. gunsmoke is thick inside the place like you bottled some factory smog.

the cops kick the door down, out billows the gunsmoke, followed by a pornographic stink.

the swat cops go in first with their shields up. with their artillery weapons in their hands and their backup pistols on their belts just in fucking case. they squint around the place. they find the assailant: a meat mountain of a man, now with swiss cheese bullet holes thru both his legs. he saved the upper half of himself, sheltered from machingun fire, by overturning and ducking under a metal catering table. a table now polka dotted with 7mm dents. rat-a-tat-tat-tat, dinner is served.

'are you armed?' comes the voice of the sergeant thru the megaphone.

dufff levels his pistol at the nearest swat cop. he cocks the hammer back to blow them away. he squints to take aim. the pistol flies out of his hand and clatters against a giant magnetic plate, held by special trooper edmunds. a gloved hand peels the gun away from the magnetic plate and disarms it ... the bullets clatter into a plastic evidence bag and are insta-stamped with today's date and a gps code of the hotdog stands exact location. the detective wearing the gloves holds dufff's gun up to the light and says 'wow ... it's a fucking antique. sheesh, you are an anachronism, aren't ya buddy?'
'sniff it' invites dufff from under the tin table.
the cops look at eachother.
'sniff it' he says again.

the cops look at eachother like 'what the?', but the detective does it. he takes the bait – and like a good police hound he has a heck of a sense of smell. he breathes deep into his nostrils, savouring the smell of the tip of the gun, inhaling it's complex aroma. the lovereek of dufff's lower intestine hits his nose like a tyson jab. bash! the detective barfs into the nearby sink.

another cop is standing knee deep in dufff's ejaculate. another one is tangled in the nautical rope. several have picked up on the sweet tang of vaginal secretions in the air.

'it smells like sex in here' says the sargeant thru the megaphone. 'well i just been jacking myself off.' says dufff. 'is why ... what else is a guy supposed to do, waiting for you slowpokes to arrive?'
two swats move in and pull him to his feet. as he stands up they see he's pantless ... misshapen cock like a peeled banana, huge ballsac swinging on empty, like pavarotti's beanbag chair.
the sargeant steps to the front of the hub-bub, swinging the megaphone. he takes in dufff's square jaw and beard made of scars, his mean mouth and dry lips and the petrol tears pooling in his bogart eyes.
'you're a dinosaur, aren't ya buddy?' says the megaphone, squelching feedback round the words, 'you're a vision of the past.' directly into dufff's face '... you're over. history. history that will be forgotten. a rusty relic. you're future, you're future is making license plates in prison ... license plates for electric cars!'
'yeah' jibes edmunds 'ya can't go too fast behind bars'

the swats hold dufff by the shoulders. across the room a pair of electric handcuffs is being removed from a foam lined briefcase, they surge like *'beeejjjsssssssssuooooo'* as they power on.
dufff watches the cuffs get passed cop to cop hand to hand making their way towards him, and thinks 'what have i got to live for now? i'd rather die a freeman by my own hand, my own way, than go down for life, and be sucking toe jam from the pinkietoes of pedophiles in prison. by my hand, my own way, and not a moment too soon ...' he pulls the pistol from the

belt of the nearest cop, levels it at his own head and squeezes
the trigger. his skull explodes like a 40 watt bulb being hit by
a baseball bat. the heat of the bullet liquifies his eyeballs, they
spray from their sockets. soaking the faces in the front row.

steaming brain drips from the walls of the hot dog stand.

homerun. dufff. back home to mother. back home to dust. dust to dust.
dufff to dust. dust. dust. dust durango.

dufff's headless torso paused for comic timing before dropping
the gun. and then froze again as if posing for a photograph. a still
life. of moving death.
it paused for comic timing, and crumpled to the floor.

the policmen wiped their eyes so they could see. dufff had
coated the entire room in the contents of his head.

detective kim rex pushed to the front of the rabble. she said 'a
moment of respect please for the fallen' and then enforced it.
she bent her shaven head down, and squeezed her eyes shut. the
other's didn't understand this behaviour but they followed suit.
the sniggering cops all respected her. so it follows they respected
her wishes. a full minute of silence and stillness was observed
for the memory of dufff durnago, a man they never met til a few
moments ago. a man who they hated on spec. a man who had
just soaked them all by exploding his own head. a man who you
and i only knew all to briefly but who we will carry a little piece
of in our hearts. ... forever.

...

cooter pink smashed a car window in with a rock. the car alarm
was blaring, its lights were flashing, the wheels and steering

column were locked down. in the year 2033, even shitty cars like the one randi rush could afford had very advanced security systems. car theft was frowned upon in the year 2033.

but cooter pink made it her business to master things that were frowned upon. and a machine is just a person that doesn't know it's a person yet, she used to say. a machine is an extension of the person who designed it, and a tool for another person to use, so if you understand both them people you got a pretty good reckoning on the machine itself. having said that, in this instance, bludgeoning the dashboard with a rock turned out to be the most time effective solution. crushing the security system without crushing the vital electronics of the engine was like performing frontal lobe lobotomy. ya gotta be careful. but ya gotta get that sucker outta there. cooter had never stolen a car before, but she'd got high and watched tutorials of other people doing it plenty. so, ya know, here goes nothing.

smash went the rock, sparks flew like fireflies. the plastic knobs of the interface fell off, but the machine was still alive. *smash* went the rock again. the lights stopped flashing and the alarm cut off abruptly to a silence like digital zero. smoke was billowing outta the dashboard. cooter stuffed her fingers into the frying holes and melting plastic to put out the electrical fire. 'now … it should just be … a case of … what exactly? … think idiot think.' she rolled the rock off her lap and outta the car. she slid across to the driving position. stared down at the digital display screens, all zeros now, backlit lizard green lcd in standby. 'think idiot think…' she tried to focus on breathing. 'be nice to yourself. breathe. yeah be nice to me. breathe. nobody likes being yelled at by you. breathe. not even me. breathe. breathe. nobody deserves to be spoken to like that. breathe. not even you deserve that. breathe. not even i deserve that.' … the division of the self was sometimes a helpful thing. having a rich interior world had its pluses. sometimes you didn't know dick about something but the other person you also were knew a little about it. 'you. just. have. to. dial. her. in.' cooter thought. she squeezed her eyes shut and tried to focussss. for a moment: nothing. eyes opened. eyes closed. again. she breathed. she breathed. she breathed and listened to it like music. she breathed. she breathed. she breathed and she began to feel waters lapping her. she breathed she breathed. she breathed she breathed and she began to wade into the waters. waters that rose around her, she breathed she breathed she lay back n let go n floated away on a pool of digital data. memories of her life mingled with things she knew to be hard fact reality hard science. swirling currents of yesteryear and tomorrow. childhood pain like icebergs, she drifted away from those towards numbers. towards knowledge. towards her own calm, sensitive, studious core. doggy paddling, and then floating on her back, buttcheeks and backs of legs to the water, nipples in the wind, she floated away from who she is in public, who others asked her to be, and towards the person she was when she was alone. totally alone. this. person. knew. this. shit. inside. out. video montages flickered in the pool, surging like electric eels, she rolled over in the water and submerged her face: saw reflections, memories, dreams, the future, the past, visual recordings of everything she'd ever seen, instruction manuals for everything she knew how to do, the instructions, the instructions, for everything she knew. the water went from cool stream to warm bath. she was one with this knowledge, one with this knowledge, and this knowledge is something we all know, she thought, the public domain, my private domain, if it is real it is here for the taking. if it is real it is reality it is here for the taking. she reached out. she reached out with an open hand. she reached in. she reached deep within herself. and. reached. the. answer.

bingo.

cooter pulls the lighter from her pocket. sparks it to check it's working. she melts plastic, strips wires and crosses them. she fumbles in her pocket. no blade in there. she opens the glove compartment and rifles inside. finds fast food wrappers, nipple clamps, and spare blades for randi's knife. good old paranoid randi. cooter unzips the pack of blades, feeds the tip of one into the screw heads. removes the lefthand panel of the dash. there is an octopus box here into which every wire is fed. she squeezes her eyes shut again to picture the colour coding of the wires. eyes open. it's dark so she has to squint to distinguish between purple and navy. she strips the purple and the orange, tangerine like her lipstick she thinks, she thinks of randi, orange lips and butterskin, where the hell is randi? she thinks of the bullet blast in the distance. and hopes it didn't kill randi. o god. she crosses the wires and melts them together with the lighter. she pulls the green wire from the socket, and melts rubber over the end. the

green wire is the security feed. she makes it a dead end. she feels
an affinity with the green wire as she does this. maybe i'm kind
of a dead end. she thinks. except i ain't dead yet. and this ain't
exactly the end.

cooter flicks the switches, the car powers on. the standby lights
glow green. if she's done it correct it'll be game on. if not, the
engine could blow. engulfing her in electric fire. probs not, they
probs don't design 'em like that anymore. fatal accidents were
frowned upon in the year 2033. but cooter pink had a soft spot
for things that were frowned upon ... cooter pink was *nothing but*
a soft spot for things that were frowned upon.

she depresses the button and the eco-engine purrs politely. after
all that drama, the noise of the engine powering on is a letdown.
'i. despise. effeminate. machines.' cooter pink thinks. she swings
her casted legs into position. the pedals are a simple forward &
stop, like a go kart, but her legs are numb and itchy and her casts
are bulky in the wheel well.
she clicks into reverse and the car pushes backwards, almost
silently. she spins it around in the clearing and takes the path out
towards the main road.
she pictures randi being rushed to safety by some of the other
petrol heads, getting squeezed into a getaway vehicle. maybe
randi was already back in the city, maybe she was worried about
cooter. maybe. maybe. cooter punches the bar's ID code into the
gps. set sights for the most likely rendezvous point, she thinks.

headlamps glare in the distance. car after car after car ... a whole
pig parade. cooter sees the lights through the gaps in the trees.
she kills her own lamps and slows the electric engine. eight
cruisers in all. they must be abandoning the scene ... they must
have classified the speedway as 'all clear'. 'ha' she thinks 'ha'.
'all clear' usually means they've made a couple arrests – they
never call off a raid empty handed. cooter bites her clementine
lips and frets over who mighta got caught. the lights disappear
and she counts 1 mississippi 2 mississippi all the way to a
hundred and a half. she peers over the dash. braves the car
forward and out onto the main road. a feeling inside her tells

her to keep her lights off. in the year 2033 it was illegal to drive without headlamps at night ... but if the troopers pull her over she'll have bigger problems than that – leg casts in a hotwired stolen car, no driving license, 3 different kinds of contraband circling her bloodstream, no state ID, a retina scan would match someone who quite clearly isn't her cause her eyeballs are second hand, and if they did a fingerprint scan they'd find she'd been wanted since she was an 11 year old dillweed with a bag of chips on each shoulder. best to keep the lights switched off, she thinks. best not to trail the cops back to civilization, she thinks. best to avoid the city, she thinks.

she powers off the gps and turns the *other way* on the main road. driving further into the nowhere.

she takes a slow speed around the perimeter of the speedway. the car battery says it's got 16 hrs worth of juice, but she's unsure her wiring job will withstand the engine turning off and then on again, so she'll have to drive crawl speed and continuous.

at the south east corner of the speedway cooter sees a flash of white flesh in the moonlight ... randi rush had waited for the commotion to die down. after she heard the cops pull out she counted to a skidillion on her toes in 5s and 10s. eventually she emerged outta the coke fridge, stepping straight into the crime scene. randi rush was trembling in the refrigerator when she heard the gun go off. she didn't know what the gun blast meant, but she knew it didn't mean anything good. and given the silence that followed, she figured it either meant that dufff was a goner, or else he'd figured out how to kill all 15 cops with just one bullet. dufff was a hell of a driver, hung like a modest horse, but little old randi hadn't had no trouble ripping the pistol from his hands, so she assumed he was no match for 15 johnny laws. she assumed ... well, kinda, sorta ... the worst. she wasn't gonna cry, though. she promised herself that. and for another thing: her body had no more fluids to give. she stepped outta the coke fridge and into the abandoned crime scene. forensics had scraped samples of durango's head splatter off the walls, but the bulk of it still clung. dripping down like cave stalactites. the hot dog stand was wrapped in police tape like a christmas present.

security cameras had been installed, drilled one into each of the four walls by special trooper edmunds. beaming a hi def signal back to screens at the station. they spotted randi when she emerged outta the fridge alright; one electric eye winked at her to get her in focus and snapped 1000 millisecond portraits, each more flattering than the last. randi didn't notice, cause she was drinking the horrid scene in. drinking it down like medicine. randi also didn't notice the tracking dart that shot out one of the cameras and lodged itself in the back of her neck. she brushed her hand across it, assumed it was a fly. or a dead spider from the coke fridge. but it was no fly! and it was no spider! it was a tracking dart … so that was randi as good as dead.

she tip-toed thru the carnage and ducked under the police tape and slipped out the door. she blinked up at the moonlight, adjusted her leathers, did an inventory of her belongings, hoping she didn't leave any traces of herself at the scene. except for the biological traces of course … but as far she knew her vaginal secretions weren't on any police files. 'and by now that's about the only place they haven't been' she thought, *har har.*

randi clipped her knife to her belt and took a slow, dazed walk towards the main road. what's the hurry? she figured. since the speedway closed a decade ago the road is basically abandoned. how long would it take her to hitch a ride back to the city? and who the fuck would pick her up? she unclipped the knife from her belt.

the gentle purr of an electric engine at bottom speed came outta the distance. 'fuzz' randi thought, 'fuck. driving without headlights. sneaky bastards, don't they know that's illegal?' randi lay flat, face first in the grass. she was too tired to run away, so she braced herself to play dead. she hoped she was invisible but if she wasn't she'd just wait til they were inches from her, roll over and slash wildly with her blade. … she heard the vehicle slow to a crawl. to a stop. an electric window buzzed open, and a voice she recognized, enthusiastic, slightly too fast, crispy like a transistor radio,

'going my way … tootsie roll?'

for emphasis cooter pink revved the electric engine. it sounded like the world's sexiest sewing machine. zzz. zzzz. Zzzzzzz.

maybe these electric cars aren't all bad, cooter thought.

& she thanked the lord who she now definitely believed in.

they drove all night, said very little.

cooter cried when she heard about dufff's demise. randi licked the
tears from cooter's face. they tasted like petrol. dufff'd been like
a brother to cooter. hell of a racer. and they'd had a dalliance of
their own once. they tied first place 10 races in a row so did the
dalliance dance to figure out who the real winner was. cooter had
come out on top. or so she said. cooter hated to lose. so she almost
never did. he'd been like a brother, cooter said, like the kind of
brother you fuck once just to verify you aren't attracted to him.

they bided their time til the morning. they hit civilization about
9am. randi showered and cried in the shower and washed her
tears down the drain and fumbled with a sore spot at the back of
her neck, a fucking bug bite she figured. that's what you get for
leaving the city.
cooter slept in randi's pajamas, slept off the overnight drive in
randi's bed. it smelled good. randi used a girly cologne called
gonorrhea coverup by urban decay.

randi was early for her 2pm shift. she worked it. and was thankful
it was uneventful.

cooter swung by to prop up the bar for the last hour or two.
and that night they finally had their date. and it turned out that
it wasn't just in cooter's head. by the end of the date? it was
everywhere. and by the morning? they were an item.

'what do you want for breakfast?' cooter asked. randi responded
my rolling her over and eating her ass like a bowl of muesli.

…

about a week later randi went for an old fashioned abortion. the
home kit she'd used the day after the race just *hadn't got it all.*
she could tell. some impulse from deep inside dufff durango was

hellbent on survival – there was so much of him up there she had to go back to the clinic three times … they kept finding more. some part of dufff really wanted to live on. some men are like that, i guess.

so randi took the fetal scrapings home to her apartment and pickled them. preserved them in formaldehyde, little chunks from dufff. and a memento of her first day at the races. she made a pair of earrings for cooter to wear and an amulet for herself. the amulet hung a bullet's distance from her petrol heart.

one night at the bar, cooter asked randi in a hushed tone, a hushed tone for cooter at least … she asked what randi thought of the petrol criminals, the speedfreaks, the adrenaline junkies, the race:

randi scrubbed the bar clean with a dirt rag and blinked those mile-long lashes, n said:
'watching you psychopaths play death games like pedal to the metal and pistons at dawn, gear sticks to the man, and caution break wind it … felt …'

cooter sucked from a tumbler of ethanol on the rocks, 'well?' she asked. 'lemme guess, lemme guess … you feel like, until now your body has not existed in this world … except as an elaborate shelf on which you carry your brain around.' she swilled her tongue around the empty tumbler.

'yeah.' said randi. 'i think i … i want in.'

'that's cause a little part of you wants *out*.' cooter said.

and they both knew it was true.

tingles ran up their spines as the tracking device beamed their exact location to a radar screen at the precinct. *beep beep beep beep*

THE MODERN SUICIDE

1.

we support people in all the other big life changes they make.
you wanna change gender? you wanna change your name? you
wanna change country? you wanna change career? you wanna
leave the abusive partner, you wanna leave the partner that you
are abusing? you wanna kick your bad habits? you wanna find
god? you wanna learn a second language? you wanna save up
for a third house? you wanna get better at foreplay? you wanna
give it all away, to charity? you wanna demolish that wall and
put on an extension? you wanna shave this, pierce that, try a set
of highlights for the summer? you wanna change the way you
vote or not vote at all? you wanna dress different, you wanna
dress down or play dress up. you wanna scale up or go down
a drize size. you wanna get back in touch with your long lost
father? you wanna find the donor? you wanna give blood? you
wanna ex-communicate your family? your therapist said it was
a good idea. you wanna excommunicate your therapist? your
family said that was a good idea. you wanna take up tai chi, or
go to thai land, just don't tie a fucking rope round your neck and
expect anybody else to understand.

cos we love life. that's what we do. we love life. we love it. we
can't get enough. of the stuff.

we suck it in we suck it in we suck it in we suck it in and most
of us pump it right back out. we suck it in we suck it we suck
it in but some of us suck at it … course that's how it is. but we
don't make allowances or accommodations for them people:
sucking at life is the ultimate handicap. our world isn't designed
for people who wish that It Didn't Exist, how could it be? *ohh*
sometimes it kinda looks like it's been designed to confirm that it
should. not … exist.

– but –

being alive is tipped WAY in favour of people who want to be
alive.

life is unfairly biased towards people who want to be alive.
it gives 'em all the advantages, to use the parlance of our ugly
time, it privileges people who wanna be alive.

the Suicidal, are the ultimate Minority ... and they're getting
more and more minor by the day

(ba-dum-chh)

cause life sucks
and some people suck at it.

ya know what being good at life is? being good at life is being
able to put up with the bullshit. being able to block out the
voices that say 'you're too good for this, babydoll ...'

being good at life is staying in an abusive relationship.

cause life sucks
and it sucks the life out of you.

2.
the modern suicide is a form of protest,
is a form of consumer revolt.
life is a product and I ain't buying it.

cancel my subscription, do not renew, i am passing on my
right of first refusal, refusing to hold up my end of the bargain,
exposing the blood and breath economy for the sham that it is.
suicide, like burning money is a sacrifice to the gods, an insult

to the gods, an imitation of the gods, depending on who you
read, a bullet blows my nose – off, travels upwards, into the hull
of my brain, a sacrifice to god, an insult to god, an imitation of
god, depending on who you, red coats the wall behind me and
the lighting rig, with the contents of my head: my memories my
thoughts my notions my secrets like mist 'do u get my goddamn
gist' my ears ring like a telephone switchboard has installed
itself in my auricle 'do u get my goddamn gist' a feedback loop,
a recording, a quotation of myself, of who I used to be, this
overheating ego, hears nothing but its own reflection, as the soul
DIES.

body crumples to the floor,

... the soul leaves the body ...
... wafts up out of the corpse ...
... it lingers in the air, taking forever to clear ...
... like a warm fart in a cold room.

and the brave amongst you do not blink from the sight,
and the perverted amongst you store these images away
on a secret harddrive in the back of your
sexdrive,
that little segment of the brain that deals with arousal
can't help notice the lump in your throat and hairs on your
hands
and the moisture in your mouth ... s
and the way *everything* is standing to attention.

and those with the fortitude for violence – the scorpios amongst
us
and those with the scorpio rising – embrace their destiny.
they clamber up onto the stage and calm the quivering coward
rest,
 who are stunned and squirming in their seats,

or else barfing into their handbags, or hiding behind their date,
– water signs mostly.

and You are among the brave,
you squat over my remains.

and you look down into the wound, into the bullethole,
squint with one eye, like you are checking for leftovers in the
fridge.
you see a few of my ½ formed thoughts …
clinging to what remains of my head …
like the last scoops of marmalade gummed
to the side of an almost empty jar.

and you scrape at it with a knife.
'uhhh … what have we got here, hon?
… evidently passed its sell-by date.'
(lick lick lick.)
'but it tastes *otay* to me!'

and everybody lines up to taste it.
and one by one y'all take it in turns to
lick the inside of my skull
til it's empty.

& later you'll say
to eachother
'that was one of the best meals i ever ate!'

(cos whether u realise it or not there's a big part of u that wants
me dead.)

this is what happens to the suicidal artiste:
that person explaining to me that life isn't worth living,
gee that really hit the spot, hearing that kinda thing
well, kinda makes my life worth living. It was so good, I cried.

and oftentimes hearing something kinda doomy and anti-life
puts these people in the mood to fuck. ... which is ... plenty
illogical.

harsh, that's very harsh
but what's so hip about *not* quitting?
we've all quit something ... crappy relationship, crappy job,
what makes this different?

kane, cobain, hemingway, brautigan, ledger, williams, wolfe,
hoffman, chestnutt, van gogh, rothko, arbus, drake, curtis,
hutchence, linkhous, emerson, gray, ackerman, ayler, debord,
deleuze, kelley, meek, plath, wallace and marilyn monroe
and that's just the ones who are staring down at me from the
bookshelves in this room as I write this.
kane, cobain, hemingway, brautigan, ledger, williams, wolfe,
hoffman, chestnutt, van gogh, rothko, arbus, drake, curtis,
hutchence, linkhous, emerson, gray, ackerman, ayler, debord,
deleuze, kelley, meek, plath, wallace and marilyn monroe
quitter quitter quitter quitter quitter quitter quitter quitter quitter
quitter quitter quitter quitter quitter quitter quitter quitter quitter
quitter quitter quitter quitter quitter quitter quitter quitter quitter
quitter

every last one of 'em.

you know what it's like to have a job you hate – either none of your co-workers realise the job sucks. or they all do but they hang in anyway …

the boss is an asshole, the customer is always right, the hours are long, they're trying to shorten our breaks, if you do some digging you find out the company we work for isn't, like, ya know, the *most* ethical, and the product we sell is designed to break just when people have come to rely on it.

so let's imagine that life is a job – which it is.
and that it's a job we all work – which we do.
lets imagine that the hours are long – which they are … they're your whole life.

and let's imagine that a lot of us is hip to the ways in which this job stinks … and the person who hates it the mostest is gonna quit. and the straw that broke the quitters back is, well, the quitter realised that if they didn't have *this* job, they wouldn't have to work a different one.
cause if life is a job, then the alternative is just do-ing *Nothing* … forever.

napping on the great couch in the sky.

SUICIDE PACT

she feels herself about to cry. starts doing the rapid blink that
dices her liquid tears into a fine mist.

braces clatter around his mouth like a second set of teeth,
providing a percussive accompaniment to everything he says. on
this occasion he says

'i'd blow my brains out in the next life faster and with less
hesitation'

and she says:

'if death is the orgasm at the end of life, i wanna be young
enough to enjoy it.'

but they both agree …
talking about death is like talking about the details of the back of
your own head.

you've never been there.
nobody lives to see that view.

you
aren't interesting.
you
aren't special.
you
aren't a good person.

unless you are … ?

but chances are you're not.

none of us are …

wait. that's too easy.
almost none of us …
but some of us, some of us, are …

& here's what you'd have to sacrifice
you'd have to give up your vanity
and your selfishness
conquer your laziness
and never be self-satisfied.

i dare you.

DEAR STRANGER

you are insecure about the wrong things

don't get me wrong ... you are right to be insecure
because there's ways in which you suck

you just can't see them

and that shit you worry so much about?
nobody else minds.

OVERHEARD ON A TRAIN

'what are you stupid? you … *actually* self-harm?
you don't have to do it, you know …
you just have to say that you do.'

YOUTH IN ASIA?

over here we do it to our old people mostly.

FREEZE YOUR HEAD

we are all killing ourselves. the question isn't are you doing it.
the question is are you doing it fast or are you doing it slow.

cigarettes, exhaust fumes, fast food, stress, microwaves, radio
signals, cell phones, laptops, stress, too many carbohydrates, too
much meat, too much sugar, no exercise, stress,

and even if you aren't actively killing yourself, you're dying
anyway.

the only people doing anything about it are the people actively
investing in the research towards immortality. for 15 thousand
they'll freeze your head. it's a lot more to freeze your whole
body. but for 15 k they'll put your head on ice and unthaw you
when the tech exists to hook ya up to a new body. i'm gonna do
a kickstarter to raise the 15 k and tell 'em I wanna be thawed out
and attached to the body of a guatamalan muscleman. imagine
it: coffee coloured zeus with this little sunburnt peanut face on
top.

but the thing is, you gotta die young or else they're gonna thaw
out your head when it's old. you'll be alive again, forever this
time, but you'll have dementia and hair plugs and bad eye sight
and dentures. you don't want them to re-animate that version …
so if you really believe that they'll find the elixir to youth, you
gotta kill yourself before you age to really benefit.

unless you think once they've cracked bringing ya back alive
and pausing agening, it'll be a cinch to master un-ageing you.
I mean imagine that … people alive forever just yo-yo-ing
back n forth from grandma to baby to grandma to baby to
grandma to baby. be like the game pong with you as the ball
and incontinence as the ping pong bats … *booo-shitmyself-booo-
shitmyself-booo-shitmyself-booo*

what happens if the company goes out of business. ya know,
before they thaw you out?

a generation from now people get enlightened, become
comfortable with ageing and dying. and this whole immortality
thing goes outta fashion,

was a late 20th century fad … they'll say … like pogs and rap-
metal.

and so the company goes outta business 100 years from now and your frozen head ends up thawing in a dumpster, getting picked over by the beaks of electronic birds.

THE KEY TO HAPPINESS

i had a key to happiness and then i lost it.
i drank too much and misplaced it.
or maybe it fell between the cracks of a sofa
or up the crack of an uber driver.

oh wait,
i found the key to happiness again
now i notice it's engraved:

if you can find something rewarding – which means you will be glad THAT you did it,
not you ARE glad while you're doing it – and other people compliment you and thank
you for doing it. then it's the right thing to do. and if you do the right thing long enough
that might just make you happy.

i'm glad all these allegations are coming to light.
not glad this shit happens
but glad it's coming to light.
cause it brings us one step closer
to a fundamental truth
about humanity
that almost nobody can see

that you and i try to ignore …

sex.

brings.

more.

bad.

into.

the.

world.

than.

good.

& i don't mean that there's more bad sex in the world than good

though … if you think back across all your relationships and one
night stands
if you rank all the fumbles n fucks you've had from best to worst
and if you could delete the bottom 51%
n replace them with good conversations,
you would, wouldn't you?

… tally up the white hot passions, the all night orgasm animal
sex
and measure it against
the faked orgasms, the pretending to enjoy it, the going thru with
it to flatter them or preserve their fragile ego, just doing it out
of a sense of duty, or because … well, what else do we have in
common anymore?

if you've done that calculation and you're still coming out in the black …

subtract any STIs, pregnancy scares, photos or videos you wish you could delete, any times you cheated or were cheated on, that threesome you were manipulated into and regretted, any times you fucked a friend and fucked up a friendship by fucking that friend, any times you've had to tell someone the feelings weren't mutual and they have to back off now, any times you made a pass at someone, got turned down, and then had to pretend you were drunk or joking or both.

wouldn't you like all the hours back that you've given to pornography?

wouldn't it be nice if your self-esteem wasn't proportional to whether or not people – or maybe just that one special person – want/s to sleep with you?

as far as i'm concerned ... your sex drive is the *worst* thing about you.

it makes you lie to your lover about where you are, so you can lie to somebody else about who you are, in order to make them your lover, and your lover your ex-lover and start the whole process again.

for a sexual victim, the fact they have a sex drive complicates their victimhood.

the dividing line between something you definitely didn't want and something you might want on a different day in a different way

… ain't always 100% crystal.

and for the sexual predator, the fact the sex drive fluctuates complicates their being a predator. the distinction between what you did and would do again and what you did that you wish you had not done, that you promise yourself you'll never ever do again …

well, let's just say it's easy to be a nice guy in the morning.

to everyone who isn't having sex with you
your sex drive makes you ugly.

imagine if there were allofasudden: no sex drive.

if it all dried up tomorrow …

before long there'd be no rape, no molestation, no pedophilia,
no abortion, no aids, no the clap, no infidelity, no pornography,
no groping on the dancefloor, no incriminating photographs
found by heartbroken partners, no secret email accounts, no
mystery stains on lapels, no chatup lines, no dinner dates, no
laughing at jokes that aren't funny, no gym socks fulls of jizz,
no lying about why the door is locked, no desk drawers with
secret compartments, no blow up dolls, no penis pumps, no
prostitution or debates about whether prostitution should be
legalised, much less shame, much less embarrassment, no push-
up bras, no cosmetics companies, no gym memberships, no
going under the knife for vanity, no more 'she was asking for it'
cause even if she begged there'd be nothing to give her.

and from now on all snuff films would be sexless.

that barely scratches the surface of the damage sex does.
what good has it ever done?

exxxactly.

but *THE WORST* thing about sex

is that it leads

directly

to …

people have this idea that i don't like babies
and that's cause i'm always saying stuff like
'i don't like babies'

or
'i hate being around babies
i hate how they're the centre of attention'

sure they're cute – but that's just your opinion,
it's not a fact like it is with a kitten.

some babies are cute, some look like they need to
go back in the oven for another twenty minutes
… is it too late to abort this one and try again?

but
i can't help think that what we're worshipping when we
gather around a baby to fawn
is ourselves. when we were younger
not you and me specifically,
but the idea of youth.
the fact we arrive on the planet
the best we're ever going to be,

when you're a baby
people travel from other countries just to meet you
even though you can't say anything yet
and they say you smell good
and ya look good even when ya don't

cause you're still an extension of the parents

(until you can talk you're just an echo of the sex that made you)

but that baby grows up to be a person
with insecurities and prejudices and
little mannerisms that make them insufferable
just like you and me.

and what kind of an ego-ist do you have to be to think that if
you made a new person out of your genetic materials, you would
actually like that person?
what if they inherited none of the 2 things you like about
yourself?
and all of the hundred and 2 you hate?

problem is …

if you don't have a baby …

you will be forced to live your own life, find meaning and
substance for yourself, not live vicariously through the little
replacements that you create.
& if you wanna leave a mark on this world you're gonna have to
do something.

uh oh …

cause maybe you ain't the type to build a monument or burn
someone else's monument to the ground. maybe you look
around and can't see anything that needs doing. and nothing
that you'd enjoy doing.
and you say *i really need to care for something, that's my mission* …

get a tamagotchi.

no, something alive …

take in a stray cat.

no, something human …

before you bring new people to the planet … why not point
yourself towards the people who are already here and make life
better for a few of them?

we got addicted, abused, abandoned, molested, we got dying,
we got left for dead, we got poor, we got lonely, we got disabled,
differently abled, we got good old fashion retarded, we got
rehabilitated, rehabili-trying my best man, we got off the wagon,
on the wagon, at risk of falling off of or up onto the wagon, we
got run over by the wagon, we got drunk driving the wagon, we
got blind, deaf, deaf-blind, blind in one eye, and double deaf, we
got deaf in both ears and deaf in one ear, we got chronic pain,
and pain in the ass, we got walks with sticks, we got so fat he
can't even walk with a stick, we got fat people and fat activism,
we got overeaters and underweight anorexics, we got binge
eaters who just can't decide which one of these teams they're on,
bulimics who are rotting their teeth with stomach acid, we got
OCD can't leave the house cause there's dirt outside, and we got
hoarders drowning in garbage, pioneering new disease cultures
from inside their apartments, we got parents with unwanted
children, and children with unwanted parents: the kind that
just won't let go, we got war veterans younger than you, we got
people protesting, saying the government should be disarmed,
we got soldiers that came back dis-armed, limbs missing, left
home for an adventure and got more than they bargained for,
we got people camped out in the streets in protest, we got people
sleeping in the streets, we got other people pretending to, in
order to ask money from you, we got charities doing what they
can, telling ya to give to them instead of the homeless, we got
people saying cut out the fucking middle man, we got shelters
and shell shocked and shell oil, we got train tracks across my

back, we got track marks, we got truthers, we got right wing and right on and we'd get a lot more done if both were gone, we got fgm and circumcision, we got stabbings and knife amnesty boxes, we got battered hookers and hookers in jail and little sachets of anthrax arriving in the mail, we got people sniffing the anthrax thinking it's coke, we got people who just can't take a joke, why's he gotta say hookers man it's 2018, we got sex workers with broken noses, activists swarming around like they're moses, we got gangrene and green eyed monsters, wake up n smell the roses, we got heart attack n heart broken, we got parts for browns n blacks but they're only there as tokens, we got 'em employed to play out the worst fears of our culture, or else they're corrective, they're saints, we got people whose destiny is to do something awful, the ramifications of which they do not understand, they're sitting in the waiting room, they're next in line, and you could do something about it if you only knew what and where to find 'em … door swings open, the indoctrination will see you now, and some of them hookers got children, the children hear the hooking through the wall, and some of them hookers got children but they're good mothers, they ain't like them others, and their children are being taken away, we got social services, anti-social behaviour, social housing, social welfare, and social people with social security who believe in social justice but don't do a goddamn thing about it, cause they so sure they're right they don't have to act, they just have to say what they believe and edit anyone different from them out, we got people blowing loads where they shouldn't and people loading up on guns to blow away the school, we got people looking the wrong way, the other way, who are in the way, looking at their own reflection in the mirror n nothing else, got people who are looking forward to the future or looking back into the past who can't keep their eyes on the present cause the present is dissolving too fast.

we got hells of every colour, and stink, leaking up from holes in the bottom of this boat, bubbling up in the sink, and clogging the throat, we got draining people that suck life out of you like vampires, we got bug eyed and bug bitten, itchy feet, itchy ass, n itchy genitals, we got don't know nothing and knows way too much, we got don't make nothing and makes way too much, we got a few people who disappear cause they don't take enough,

and way more of us taking way too much. there's gave up. but
there's no such thing as gave enough.

take away the suffering of people
who already exist

don't medicate yourself
by needlessly bringing more
people into existence.

people who don't even have
a mouth with which to say
No Thankyou.

and if all the world's problems
are beneath you
and you won't be fulfilled until
you see your fingerprints
allover a child

… adopt.

howsabout you help clean up someone else's mess
instead of creating a mess of your own?

and if you want a kid
but you aren't willing
to care for one
that is already alive …

'not my problem'

then I pity the child you'll have.

(you pillar of the community, you)

and if you insist on having
your own
and you only love them
because they're your own
then know this …

your love for your children
is the socially acceptable version
of smelling your own farts.

you want to play god?
you want to create life?
breed puppies.

and then give them to the homeless.
homeless people with dogs get more donations.

if *nobody* had babies,
if we stopped replacing ourselves
the species would die out.

do you think the animals would mind?

the planet? would she shed a tear?

the rainforests and the ozone layer would not mind
the icecaps would not mind

IF THE HUMAN RACE WERE TO LET ITSELF GO EXTINCT

(PLANNED OBSOLESCENCE)

just think of the next 100 years we could have
if we made the next 100 years our last 100 years
'but we gotta leave this planet inhabitable for our children'
('and their children and their children')

not if we don't have any, not if none of us do,

if people born today were the last people born

imagine old age, how good it would be, with the world
population shrinking
more stuff to go around, so much food and shelter it'd be like we
was kids at a theme park in the off season.

and we'd be the last humans …

and the first ones to admit
(en masse)
that human life
(en masse)
isn't a good thing.

we'd be the climax, we'd be the headliners.
the last song before the credits roll
before the slow fade to black.

we could go out with such a bang
we could do our worst on this planet
and then disappear
we wouldn't leave a dent.
we could treat this planet like we
jumped the fence into a keg party
at the playboy mansion …

we could burn styrofoam just for fun, we could send rockets
into space to bring back those balls of trash that we fired out
there and then dropkick them into the rain forest, we could
modify cars so they burn *more* fuel. when ya get home at night
you could winch your car up like a mechanic does and put a
brick on the gas pedal so the engine runs all night. we could
send explosive experts into dormant volcanoes to light their
wicks, pump the ash into the atmosphere. we could re-activate
chernobyl, tear down the world's tallest skyscrapers and hollow
'em out n sew 'em all together into one huge pipe, place one
end over chernobyl and the other end up into the sky, focus all
that nuclear radiation directly at what's left of the ozone layer.
we could empty the great lakes and refill 'em with coca-cola. we
could prize open our landfills like the overstuffed closets they
are, let all our skeletons out, a centuries worth of buried trash
oozing onto the landscape. dig up all the remaining fossil fuels,
burn 'em for no reason, as a sacrifice to the gods, as an insult to
the gods, as an imitation of the gods,

we could hire the best living poets – the shakespeares of our
age – to compose the perfect suicide note. and then scrawl this
perfectly worded note across the face of the planet, maybe pave
over a desert in concrete and paint it white with aerosol spray
cans and then take all the crude oil we got left and put it in a
massive ink well, create a quill out of the carcasses of all the
endangered birds we can round up. and cursive out this perfect
note with the wording just so, *on behalf of our entire species, on
behalf of our entire species we say we say goodnight*, the writing would
be all curly q and meticulous penmanship, like they teach you
in grade school, careful to dot all the me's and cross all the
cucifixes, and we'd sign it from all of us, all of us who had ever
lived, everybody's name, anybody who'd ever lived would be at
the bottom of this goddamn thing.

AND

if there's any crude oil left, we load up the last lorries and
transport trucks. drive 'em at low speed in a high gear, a huge
convoy, weaving our way, taking the scenic route, all the way
up north, north of the border, north of the tree line, north into
pure nature, past the inuit towns where everybody got hooked
on crack, past the frozen waterfalls, past the nuclear test site,

past the tin shed with the painter doing paintings of the snowy
landscape (coulda just bought a pack of blank white paper and
saved himself the time), past the abandoned military outpost,
past the last airport, past the tribe who worship a tub of ben
and jerry's as their god, past the last igloo settlements, past the
climate change protesters frozen dead in a block of ice, past
santa clause, mrs clause, rudolf et al … and
CLANK.
you dent the front end of your truck against that stripy red and
white pole.
and from here
(at the top of the world)
you look out to outer space, and see the stardust that all us dead
people have gone back to being. and you pour the last drops
of crude oil directly onto the polar ice caps like you're frosting
cupcakes, and then ya light it on fire, like flambé.

and these food analogies are appropriate because death is the
dessert at the end of life.

and as the flames burn, and the last humans die one by one til
there's nobody left, the earth will breathe a sigh of relief and
she'll say … *is that all you fuckers got?*

who's the top of the foodchain now, bitch?

SUICIDE PACT (REPRISE)

death is like the back of your own head
you've only seen it in reflections
and in the occasional dream.

I VACUUM'D UP THE STARDUST

i vacuum'd up the stardust

i discriminated against a black hole

i passed an asteroid like a gallstone

i was weaned on the titties of the milky way

i took a big shit in the little dipper
hung myself with orion's belt
i was the 2nd gunman in the assassination of a shooting star

i taught kike jokes to jew-piter
played the devil's chord to mars
i sung off key to nep-tune
and stood up when sat-urn rolled in

i popped a pill and came up with the sun
came too soon with the moon
i blinked and missed her eclipse
as she wiped me from her lips
not that it matters cause out in space nobody can hear you
cream
i can prove the russians got to her first, man, if there was a space
race them ruskies won it, 1965

i plunged my thermometer deep into mercury
flipped you over, put you into gear and took ur-anus for a drive
i doubled back on myself
i told the sun he was illegitimate
i flashed my ass at the moon
we drove out to the wrong side of the sky
and pawned saturn's rings
i used the $ to get my nipples pierced

giant metal spike straight thru
the areola borealis

i flagrantly ignored your solar system
i did not allow you to planet

i told these goofy jokes to pluto,
and ya know who did not laugh?
the dog. star. sirius.
so my boner taught him to fetch
RAUW   RAUW   RAUW
bow wow wow wow

i called the lightyears fat minutes
i told mer-cure-y it's terminal
no hope no hope no hope no hope

i praised thatcher to the northern lights
made armstrong kneel
and put two fingers in my NASA
i fucked you in your ass-tronauts

i'm a rebel without a cosmos
and i'm here to get dirty
with earth

now who snorted all the stardust?

DAIRY MILK (REPRISE)

dairy milk drag queens, sucking breast milkshakes, in the
parking lot of an upstate dairy queen. chem trails streak the sky
above us, like toxic money shots at the climax of a government
porno for military mind control.

'don't you breathe it in faggot' you say 'that's how *they* get you.'
we three drag queens take long drags of mentholated charcoal.
we are yellow stained middle fingers.

broken promises dribble off my chin, pooling with ice cream
lipstick in my lap.

as night arrives to save us – night arrives on horseback – and
night pulls out and frignatures his way all across the whore's
back – the last embers of my suburban sun tan flicker goodnight
& SOS from heaven

all the way to right here.

we 3 drag queens are square jaws and stubbly legs, dressed to
9/11's .

in illegal-high-heels and screaming low cut dresses with
sunflower patterns.

sunflowers with open mouths shouting 'i may not be in fashion
this season rick but i cling to a man's cleavage like disease clings
to his speckled dick'

and i wish i were an angel, doc, i wish i were dead.

cause i'd float up from this tailgate party, thru the sky, huffing
chem trails all the way, having chem sex with an angel or 2 in
the queue for st peter's check in desk …

'i'm glad to be dead, st penis'

i'd say.

tipping my halo like a hat …

'frankly, i couldn't wait to die

cause it's just one thing after another

with those goddamn humans.'

KISSING THE SHOTGUN GOODNIGHT
I

streaking comets, a trail of smoke and fire
streaking comets, a trail of smoke and fire
streaking
streaking comets

set your controls for right here
set your controls

you wake up
you wake up
you wake up and realise
you are not alone
you are host to a parasite
you wake up, you wake up
and it wakes up inside of you

she ripped the needle out of her arm
she ripped the needles out of her arms
she ripped the needles out of her arm,
kicked the hospital bed over
and scrambled out of that fucking scene.

she wipes the devil's blood from her mouth
she'd only been back in her earth body 12 minutes
and already she's back on the job.

she'd only been back in her earth body 12 minutes, in her earth
body

suck the poison off my lips
suck the poison off my lips
suck the poison off my lips
suck the poison off my lips

suck the poison off my lips x 2

mouthpiece
mouthpiece
mouthpiece
mouthpiece
mouth at peace
mouth at peace
mouthpiece
mouth
put the piece in your mouth
put the piece in your mouth
piece of your mouth
of your mouth. of. piece.
put a piece of your mouth on a piece of my mouth
i put a piece of you
a piece of you
in my mouth, in my mouth
and pull back the hammer.

click.
gone.
sucked out of the body like a air hostess
when the cabin door is ripped open
in a lightning storm.

click.
gone.
sucked out of the body like a air hostess
when the cabin door is ripped off.

click.
gone.

open mouth to eat. open mouth to scream.
open mouth to load a gun in.

open mouth to eat. open mouth.
open mouth to blow the load of a gun in.

you awake from a hell dream, from a god dream, from a kanye
dream. from a succession of kerosene wet dreams where you
and steve albini spit roast a ghost.

you awake from a dream of psycho-masturbation, of aberrations,
of perversions, of eroto-maniacal satanic pathology, of
turbulent kisses and tender seas. of mammary worship. of
posterior worship. of genital worship. the holy trinity. a racial
scream, a medical outcry, a discordant racket, the throaty
cries and infantile fixations of a primordial … you awake to
the acceptance that you are primitive … and this, this is an
intellectual vacuum.

and tinnitus never sounded so good.
tinnitus never sounded.

a muzzle
a muzzle
a muzzle
a candle sprouting arms to snuff itself out
a candle sprouting arms to snuff itself out
a candle burns itself a mouth
to blow itself
out.

squirt two new people out
squirt two new people out
squirt two new people out
you and her, you and him,
decide
squirt out two new people
squirt them out
they are in you
squirt them out

they are in you
squirt two new people out
squirt
squirt
squirt two new people out

your chest is prized open by a fork of lightning
by a fork
your chest
your chest is prized open by a fork of lightning
jump rope with your lower intestine
jump rope with your lower intestine
doing double dutch just to taunt god
doing double dutch just to taunt god
doing double dutch
just to taunt him.

we don't know what we are
we don't know what we are
we don't know what we are
we don't know what we are
we don't know what we are
we don't know what we are
what don't know what we are
what don't know what we are
what don't know what we
what don't know what we are
what don't know what we
what don't know what
don't know what we are
don't know what we are
don't know what we are
we don't know what we are
we don't know what we are
we don't know
we don't know

we don't know
what
we are
we are

you are a crayola deathwish
a deathwish written in crayon
a deathwish in crayola

the difference a comma makes:
do you wanna smoke some crack baby?

earthbound missile . earthbound missile .

the difference a comma makes:
do you wanna smoke some crack, baby?
the difference a comma makes:
do you wanna smoke some crackbaby?

will the end of the world be a bad thing?
might be kinda interesting to live through, might be kinda fun,
not just from a karma retribution POV, actual day-2-day,
minute-2-minute fun
fun, fun, fun, fun,
to watch.

i will not be having a baby
i do not believe there will be anything worth living for by the
time it could walk
walk, walk,
i will not be having a baby
squirt
squirt
squirt

image: woman points a gun at her pregnant bump
'you think i don't take our future seriously?'

messiah complex
messiah complex
messiah complex – it's simple
it's simple:
you will die and come back a battery farm chicken
it's simple:
you will die and come back a battery farm chicken
you will die and come back a battery farm chicken
i hope you …
you will die and come back a battery farm chicken
a battery
a battery
you will die and come back a battery
a battery a battery a battery
assault
assault and battery, chicken.

the buck stops here the buck stops
here the buck stops here the fucks
stop here the fucks stop here the
buck stops here::::::::::::::
no more life from these loins
onward and onward and onward
no more.

just cause you don't care doesn't mean it doesn't matter
just cause you don't care doesn't mean it doesn't matter
just cause you don't care doesn't mean it doesn't matter
just cause you don't care doesn't mean it doesn't
just cause you don't care doesn't
just cause you care doesn't mean it doesn't matter
just cause you care doesn't mean it doesn't matter

just cause you care doesn't mean it doesn't matter
just cause you care doesn't mean it matters
just cause you care doesn't mean it matters
just cause you care doesn't mean it

KISSING THE SHOTGUN GOODNIGHT
2

we sleep on a chainlink bed
with petrol tears in our screensaver eyes.
a hyde of leatherette is stretched taut
over our fibreglass ribcage.

embers of the last love ever flicker goodnight
the sweat fever sleep of a hell dream

'this is a hell dream' you whisper and you grasp out.
you are sleeptalking into a telephone receiver.
cold snot dries in our breathing holes.

'if we ever wake up, we are leaving this goddamn planet.'

the firmament had sprung a leak, the sun had frozen over,
the best of us were dead or dying. where the speed freaks and
junkies come to cum and die. by petroleum fumes and burning
tires, one by one the adrenaline junkies come to the speedway to
die.

and who wants to go out with a full deck?

one last bolt of adrenaline. one more race. chasing that first.
ever. high.
pedal down. pushed into the seatback. no airbag in front of
me. because if i'm dying by impalement on a steering column
tonight i'm doing under a freeman's moon.

'this is a hell dream'
'this is a hell dream'

you better hope there's free beds at the morgue tonight cause
we're gonna need 'em ...

'this is a hell dream' you say.
grasping out in the night.
sleeptalking into a telephone receiver.
cold snot drying in your breathing holes.

if we ever wake up
we are leaving this goddamn planet.
if we ever wake up.

you wake up, you wake up,
you wake up, and realise.
you wake up and realise
you are not alone.
you are host to a parasite.
there is someone growing inside of you.

you wake up, you wake up,
and it wakes up inside of you.

you rip the needles out of your arms.
you kick the hospital bed over
and scramble out of that scene.

you wipe the devil's blood from your mouth.
you've only been back in your earth body 12 minutes.

brace brace.
brace brace.
brace brace.

your skull is the cockpit.
the pilot has switched off the fasten seatbelt sign again.
we are falling through clouds.
when you hear brace brace brace brace
you try not to chatter your teeth right out of your skull.
brace brace.
you adopt the position: you put the mask over your mouth.
you breathe deep
into the yellow plastic cup
that is strapped to your face.
you try not to snap
the elastic as you wrap the bag around your head

and you whisper
'it won't end like this, i promise. don't dwell on this ... you'll
develop a fetish.'

can you taste the storm?
commuter train. computer train.
commuter train. a savage kneels,
draws a dotted line on the back of his own neck, careful to get a
neat kill. cause there's decorum in war and a hero never arrives
at the lips of hell. a hero never got bad breath or bad brains.
stolen cloud nothing delivers heaven on a plate to those who
deserve it, to those who have earned it.

i hear no sound but the blood rushing to my brain *(gunshot)*
you hear no sound but the blood rushing to your brain ...

& cloud king nada eats shit, licks lips,
like a standing stage treated like a box of soap.
he is treating his stage like a box of soap.
a suicide note is tattoo'd on your throat
since the day you got born.
we wrote a song:we sung of dystopia, we were off topic. we were
a throttled rocket.
we blew a message of 'means nothing' across your heart
like militant rebel shits
scrawled in police gag swagger, a cartoon noose.
and let's one thing be as clear as crystal: those people wanted
to die. you telling 'em they shouldn't, that their life is worth
something. to you maybe it is. you got no idea what it was like
to walk to the fridge in their shoes let alone a whole mile ... now
who's selfish?

you spoke slow, you spoke slow as if you were coining each
word ...

'motor. yard. oleander.'
smudges under my eyes as dark as a mechanics grease.
blood foaming from your mouth … you've bitten off your own
tongue again.
a long arm from the future is reaching back, reaching back
with an open hand to grasp the opportunity for life. planting an
impulse in his brain to not. pull. out.
he passed a white brick into her.
a million side-chained sperms,
as thick n gelatinous as …
a whole hospitals worth of gal stones
in one heroic … 'unghh'

you fire a cylinder into the brain,
you eliminate the master. the master who
has made a kangaroo courtroom inside your temple.
you are hung like a good jury.
you bounce a coin: heads you lose.
brains blown apart inside of a plastic bag.

i'm riding riptide on a rocket straight to your heart,
straddling and strapped in,
burrowing into a hole of ripped flesh
fresh in the face.
gasoline burns internal as the bullet travels your veins.
bottlenecking by a blood clot, skid marks on a body rot,
oceans of muscle,
vistas of pain
bubbling like froth from a boxer's split lip.

cut the cord from the mains: this brain has been dead for years.

you feel a pin prick.

the electric lights warble. wave after wave of

excruciating nausea. stomachs flip and empty their contents.

the sensation is like sitting forward, sitting forward and falling out,

forward, forward, falling out of your chair.

your earth body stays chained to the stretcher

lifes leave it

(chh ...)

life leaves it. limp.

you are not a simulation of a corpse, but in that moment ...

the real thing.

your astral body, your soul,

shoots out the bodies waste pipe as a gas.

you experience this as a vision.

closing in from the corners,

narrowing to a pin prick, to a circle,

to a tunnel of light

into which you drift, you float.

a dark blue tunnel surrounds you,

pulsing like a hollowed out snake.

and through this portal you access

the great beyond,

the great below,

the great above,

heaven, hell, purgatory,

the next life,

the last life.

you pass first into the western lands, the land of the recently
dead, where by looking left and right, you smudge your face
to the train window ... you see the recently dead, those who
you have recently lost. many get stuck here, choosing them
over their friends and family who still walk the earth. they let
their time run out on kevorkian's clock. they stray too far from

his transmission, they can't find their way home. they permit
themselves to die for real.

you've got an airbag in your chest.
you are held together by medical metal.
the crash didn't kill you.
you've got an airbag in your chest in case it happens again.
a metal plate is reinforcing every flat surface of your body.
you have a row of false teeth behind your real ones.
you've got a wig of your own hair in a closet at home …
your scalp, your flesh was burned off
when the engine exploded.

the firmament had sprung a leak,
the sun had frozen over,
the best of us were dead or dying.

we stand. each of us holding our battered face up for judgement.
limbs missing. the occasional eyeball swinging from a socket.
it's nothing that cannot be repaired,
nothing that can't be replaced,
nothing we can't learn to live without.

we are blood spattered wrecks
cooling in the frozen sun
and we wear our battle scars
and our broken blood vessels
with pride.

unable to think. to move.

in words. do not think in words.
do not think in thoughts.
do not think in words
do not think in thoughts.
do not travel
even as far as the end of this sentence.

live tour credits:

dramaturg & creative producer: **anne rieger**
producer & general manager: **beckie darlington**

thanks to anne for helping sift thru all this shit (and suffering through the parts that got cut) and thanks to beckie for booking the tour and answering a bazillion emails.

supported by arts council england. commissioned by theatre in the mill. support from ARC stockton arts centre, the marlborough theatre and shoreditch town hall.

by the same author:

THIS IS HOW WE DIE

available from the fine people at oberon books
or from the web store at
www.christopherbrettbailey.com